I CAN'T STOP THINKING ABOUT VAR

I CAN'T STOP
THINKING ABOUT VAR

DAISY CHRISTODOULOU

Swift

SWIFT PRESS

First published in Great Britain by Swift Press 2024

1 3 5 7 9 8 6 4 2

Copyright © Daisy Christodoulou, 2024

Printed and bound in Great Britain by CPI Group (UK) Ltd,
Croydon CRO 4YY

A CIP catalogue record for this book is available from the
British Library

ISBN: 9781800754935
eISBN: 9781800754942

Dedication TK

There rolls the deep where grew the tree.
    O earth, what changes hast thou seen!
    There where the long street roars, hath been
The stillness of the central sea.

The hills are shadows, and they flow
    From form to form, and nothing stands;
    They melt like mist, the solid lands,
Like clouds they shape themselves and go.

But in my spirit will I dwell,
    And dream my dream, and hold it true;
    For tho' my lips may breathe adieu,
I cannot think the thing farewell.

'In Memoriam'
Alfred Tennyson

CONTENTS

FOREWORD

JONATHAN WILSON

It was in Düsseldorf that the revelation struck. I'd been invited over by the local tourist board before the Euros and been taken to Fortuna against Greuther Fürth in 2.Bundesliga. In the second half, a Fortuna player seemed to have scored a brilliant overhead kick, the sort of goal that gets you to your feet even if you have no investment in the game. But it became apparent something was wrong. The players had not gone back to their own halves. They were hanging around, waiting. Everybody waited. For four or five minutes nothing happened. Then the referee thrust his arm into the air: no goal.

To be honest, I hadn't even realised they had VAR in 2.Bundesliga. Which was when it hit me I go to probably around 80 matches a season for work and pleasure, but this was the first time I'd ever been to a game in which VAR was in operation but I wasn't in the press box. I had no screen look at. There were no replays visible to me. I looked on social media, but nobody on my feed was talking about Fortuna Düsseldorf v Greuther Fürth, let alone uploading replays. For those four or five minutes, I had no idea what was going on. I chatted with the people around me. What were they checking? There was nothing obvious. The player who had executed the overhead was definitely onside. There had been no apparent contact between players, no handball. Eventually, trying to play back the action in our minds, we deduced the issue must have come when the ball was initially played wide, 15 or 20 seconds before the goal. Had there been an offside then?

I still don't know for sure, but that's a best guess. Offside was given, although the free-kick was taken from a more central position. And that was when it really dawned on me: VAR, in its current form, is terrible, at least in terms of the in-stadium experience.

A few months earlier, I'd been in Sweden, the only one of Europe's 30 highest-ranked leagues not to have adopted VAR. As the financial structures of modern football have increasingly shut their teams off from the sort of European achievement enjoyed by Malmö and IFK Gothenburg in the seventies and eighties, Swedish football has begun to market itself as a fans' paradise, a place that retains a traditional football feel. That itself is a contested notion, given the excesses and self-importance of many ultra groups, but one area of unanimity among fans is their opposition to VAR.

My attitude at the time hadn't really changed from a decade earlier, when I'd thought VAR desirable in principle but was unconvinced about how it could be implemented. What talking to Swedish fans made me realise was the extent to which VAR is a phenomenon that exists because of television fans who, seeing replays of errors within a few seconds, are much less tolerant of them than those in the stadium who might not learn a decision is wrong until several hours later. (As phones, networks and stadium WiFi improve, those two groups may converge.)

That slightly hardened me against VAR, if only for reasons of nostalgia. It's impossible not to be aware as I approach fifty of how the experience of the game has changed since I was a child and, sport being an inherently conservative activity, resisting that. Just as I essentially think that kits should look like they did in the eighties, so I have a sense that kids should get into football in the way I did: by paying their £2.50 every week to stand on a terrace. Whatever was miserable about that experience – and much was, from the rain to the undertone of danger to the abysmal football being played – it did at least foster a sense of community, an indelible identification with place. Most of my relationship with home is mediated through football. Although far more fans these days watch in television than go to the ground, I still instinctively privilege match-going fans.

But it was only in Düsseldorf I realised just how dreadful the in-stadium experience of VAR is if you're not sitting in a press-box with a monitor in the desk next to you. VAR has since come to seem a symbol of the general contempt with which football's authorities treat match-going fans.

Does that mean I'm opposed to it? No. Not in principle. The problem is that it was imposed as a fait accompli for the 2018 World Cup with next to no consultation either as to whether it was desirable, or as to what form it should take. That it might expose grey areas in the existing laws seems to have occurred to no one.

Nobody had done what this book does, which is to lay out the various issues and compromises involved with VAR, using expertise from other fields, asking what exactly we want the game to look like and proposing a framework of how we might get to a workable model.

Over the past six years, I've read and discussed VAR so much the tendency is for my eyes to glaze over. Daisy's achievement has been to open my eyes again and make me think, 'Yes, this is the debate we should have been having all along.'

INTRODUCTION

FRANCE VS REPUBLIC OF IRELAND, 18 NOVEMBER 2009

It's extra time in the second leg of a World Cup qualifier play-off. France and Ireland are tied at 1–1 over the two legs of the match, and there are just 17 minutes to go before the game goes to penalties. If Ireland win, it will mean they qualify for their first World Cup in 16 years. Florent Malouda sends a long free kick into the Irish penalty area. It looks as if he has over-hit it and that the ball will go out for a goal kick. But somehow, the talismanic French forward Thierry Henry keeps the ball in and then crosses it for his teammate William Gallas to score.

The French players run away celebrating, but the Irish players are just as animated. They surround the referee, tapping their hands, signalling that Henry used his hand to control the ball and stop it going out. A few seconds later, fans at home can see exactly what they mean. The slow-motion replay shows that Henry was only able to keep the ball in by handling it – not just once, but twice. The referee, Martin Hansson, doesn't seem to have had a great view of what has happened. He was standing at the other edge of the penalty area, and there are a few players in between him and Henry who probably blocked his line of sight.

The Irish players protest and protest, but the referee has awarded the goal and there is nothing that can be done to change the decision.

This incident has far-reaching implications. Many other sports have introduced some form of decision review system to help officials make difficult judgement calls. Football is an outlier. FIFA, the game's governing body, has resisted the introduction of technology, saying it would interrupt the natural flow of the game.

But it is a stance that is increasingly difficult to justify. Of course, referees have always made mistakes – Henry's handball draws instant comparisons with Diego Maradona's infamous 'Hand of God' goal from the 1986 World Cup – but in 2009, technology is reshaping the way the whole world works. Fans at home and in the ground can instantly see replays and commentary on their TVs and smartphones. Other sports are embracing the opportunities of technology. Younger fans simply don't understand why you can't easily overrule such an obvious howler. It feels like a watershed moment, one where the increasing pressure for change finally makes a hidebound institution crack. Some form of technological decision review system feels inevitable.

GERMANY VS DENMARK, 29 JUNE 2024

It's just after half-time in the Euro 2024 match between the hosts, Germany, and Denmark. David Raum chases down a loose ball on the left wing and attempts to cross into the Danish box, but it's blocked by Joachim Andersen and the ball goes out for a corner.

Michael Oliver is the on-field referee, and unlike Martin Hansson in 2009, he has the support of technology. There is another official, a video assistant referee (VAR), who is watching the match on a screen and can tell the on-field referee if there are any decisions he should review. In this case, the VAR tells Oliver to look again at Andersen's block. Oliver reviews the incident on a screen at the side of the pitch and decides that Andersen has blocked the ball with his hand. It's therefore a penalty. He's helped in his decision by a 'snickometer', a sensor placed in the ball which shows that Andersen did indeed handle it.

But while the ball may have touched Andersen's hand, most pundits and ex-players are left frustrated by the decision. Andersen was running at speed, trying to get back and defend. He is incredibly close to the ball when Raum hits it. He does turn his body, attempting to block the cross with his back, but the ball is hit at pace and it catches him on the arm. It's hard to see how he could have avoided it. He has not gained much advantage from the action, and it feels incredibly harsh to penalise his team with a penalty. Denmark go on to lose the game 2–0 and are knocked out of the tournament.

By now we are so used to inexplicable VAR decisions that ITV have employed a specialist referee and lawyer, Christina Unkel, to attempt to make sense of them. She does a good job of explaining why the laws mean we have ended up in this place. But she does not convince anyone that the outcome makes any kind of sense. The relevant section of the law is as follows:

It is an offence if a player touches the ball with their hand / arm when it has made their body unnaturally bigger. A player is considered to have made their body unnaturally bigger when the position of their hand / arm is not a consequence of, or justifiable by, the player's body movement for that specific situation. By having their hand / arm in such a position, the player takes a risk of their hand / arm being hit by the ball and being penalised.

The judgement is that Andersen has made his body unnaturally bigger in a way that is not justifiable by his movement. But he is running. People do move their arms away from their bodies when they are running. It would be more unnatural if they didn't.

While the pundits are frustrated, they are not surprised. This is not the first time that the VAR system has led to a result that seems completely opposed to any notion of common sense. The commentator, Clive Tyldesley, concludes by saying, 'The handball rule should be written for the whole game, not for VAR. Don't force a schoolteacher to tell a nine-year-old boy or girl that their body silhouette was unnatural. There's no snickometer on the playing field. It's orange-juice time. Rip it up and start again.'

VAR was meant to solve glaring errors like the Henry handball, but it has ended up being used to create handball offences that previously may never even have been spotted, let alone penalised. Many fans, players and managers are sick to death of it. It's been used in the Premier League since 2019, but far from overcoming its teething problems, its flaws seem only to have increased over time. Wolverhampton Wanderers were so frustrated with VAR's performance in the 2023–24 season that they asked for a vote on getting rid of it. In 2024, Sweden became the only one of the top 30 leagues in Europe to reject its use. Fans in Norway dislike the system so much that they have started throwing Danish pastries and fishcakes onto the pitch in protest.

Similarly, by the summer of 2024, the wider debate about technology and authority is much darker than it was in 2009. In 2009, the iPhone was a glorious new piece of technology, and a fresh-faced Mark Zuckerberg was promising that Facebook would bring the world closer together. Smartphones and social media were going to deliver a new era of connection, prosperity and entertainment. By 2024, however, the mood is different. Technology companies are being blamed for disinformation, election interference, low-quality jobs and mental-health crises. The big new debate in technology isn't about which new social media start-up is the coolest, but rather whether artificial intelligence is going to destroy us or if it's just a giant con. Apocalypse or trillion-dollar grift: take your pick.

It's hard not to see the persistent and seemingly unfixable woes of VAR as a symbol for wider technological hubris and overreach. In 2009, using technology in sport felt inevitable in a good way, like it was on the right side of history. In 2024, it still feels inevitable, but more in the way that the eventual collapse of the universe into a black hole is inevitable.

What on earth went wrong? How has something that should have been such a simple improvement ended up causing so much controversy and unhappiness? And is there any way we can fix it?

PART 1
PROBLEMS

1

HANDBALL

'If the rule you followed brought you to this,
of what use was the rule?'

Cormac McCarthy, *No Country for Old Men*

THE SPIRIT OF THE LAW LEADS TO INCONSISTENCY

It is obvious why the handball law exists. If you don't have a law about handball, you don't have football. When football players break this law, as William Webb-Ellis is alleged to have done in 1823, they aren't playing football any more.

Before VAR, the handball law was quite simple. It was just 20 words long, as follows:

Handling the ball involves a deliberate act of a player making contact with the ball with the hand or arm.

There were three bullet points clarifying what 'deliberate' meant, but these were advisory. It was a law that gave referees a lot of discretion.

Discretionary laws rely on a shared understanding of the spirit of the law. They work on the basis that everyone – players, referees, fans – has a common-sense understanding of what the law should be, and they give the referee latitude to use their discretion to make decisions about what does and does not infringe it.

In some ways, this approach can work well, but its major problem is inconsistency. Different referees will interpret laws in different ways, and even the same referee might judge two quite similar incidents differently. When that happens in the same match, it's hugely controversial.

Inconsistency is a threat to the integrity of any authority. If we are going to be penalised for not following laws, then we want to know exactly what the laws are and what we have to do to avoid being penalised. Players and managers develop tactics and strategies designed to work within the laws. If they can't be certain about how the laws will be interpreted, it makes that job much harder.

Inconsistency is also a problem, because it frequently leads to accusations of bias: how come this team gets marginal handball calls in its favour, and that team doesn't?

When you see how attempts to enforce consistency go wrong, it is easy to criticise them as pedantic, bureaucratic nonsense. But the impulse to improve consistency is not nonsense; it is something that most fans care deeply about, and it goes to the heart of issues about fairness.

The other problem with the old handball law was the one bit of specific guidance it did give: that a handball had to be 'deliberate' to be an offence. Often it was hard to know when a handball was deliberate, and players could still get big advantages from accidental handballs. One famous example was Laurent Koscielny's last-minute winner for Arsenal against Burnley in 2016. Koscielny mis-kicked the ball, which flew up, hit him on the hand and went into the goal. It was definitely accidental, as it all happened so quickly there was no time for any deliberation. But something about the decision felt wrong, as it would never have been a goal if the ball hadn't hit his hand. In the 2018–19 season, there were other high-profile accidental handball goals from Willy Boly, Alexandre Lacazette and Sergio Agüero.

Incidents like this have been happening since football began. But improved TV coverage brings more scrutiny by pundits and fans. A video review system increases this scrutiny, and it's hard to sustain a discretionary law when incidents can be pored over and replayed in such detail.

At the same time as video review systems were being trialled, changes to the handball law were being discussed too. In 2019–20, a new handball law and new video assistant referee system were introduced into the Premier League at the same time. The VAR system had been used in other competitions, including the World Cup and Champions League, in previous seasons, but the handball law was new for everyone and had been developed by the International Football Association Board (IFAB), who set the laws of football.

This is what the law became in 2019–20:

It is an offence if a player:

- deliberately touches the ball with their hand/arm, including moving the hand/arm towards the ball
- gains possession/control of the ball after it has touched their hand/arm and then:
  - scores in the opponents' goal
  - creates a goal-scoring opportunity
- scores in the opponents' goal directly from their hand/arm, even if accidental, including by the goalkeeper

It is usually an offence if a player:

- touches the ball with their hand/arm when:
  - the hand/arm has made their body unnaturally bigger
  - the hand/arm is above/beyond their shoulder level (unless the player deliberately plays the ball which then touches their hand/arm)

The above offences apply even if the ball touches a player's hand/arm directly from the head or body (including the foot) of another player who is close.

Except for the above offences, it is not usually an offence if the ball touches a player's hand/arm:

- directly from the player's own head or body (including the foot)
- directly from the head or body (including the foot) of another player who is close
- if the hand/arm is close to the body and does not make the body unnaturally bigger
- when a player falls and the hand/arm is between the body and the ground to support the body, but not extended laterally or vertically away from the body

This law is 11 times longer than the previous one and does not rely on an understanding of the 'spirit of the law'. It's the opposite: a 'letter of the law' approach that reduces discretion and judgement and attempts to precisely define all the possible ways a ball can strike a hand.

It was a bit of a coincidence that the new handball law and VAR were introduced into the Premier League in the same season. But in another way, the two are closely linked. The changes to the handball law would have been impossible to implement without some form of slow-motion replay and scrutiny. Likewise, once you introduce a video review system, it's much harder to maintain a discretionary law. Referees, players and fans are going to want more guidance.

THE LETTER OF THE LAW LEADS TO ABSURDITIES

But if the spirit of the law leads to inconsistencies, the letter of the law leads to absurdities.

In the first week of the 2019–20 season, VAR and the new handball law were immediately in the spotlight. Leander Dendoncker thought he had scored for Wolves against Leicester, but the goal was overturned by the video assistant referee, who spotted a handball by Willy Boly in the build-up.

A week later, something similar happened. Gabriel Jesus thought he had scored a last-minute winner for Manchester City against Spurs. But the goal was reviewed, and it turned out that his teammate Aymeric Laporte had touched the ball with his hand in the build-up.

In both cases, the handballs were accidental. Under the previous law, therefore, they would not have been penalised. But under the new one, accidental handballs that lead to goals are an infringement. In a pre-VAR world, it would have been highly unlikely that either handball was noticed in real time. You need the slow-motion scrutiny of VAR to spot the offence. These were textbook examples of the new law and the new video system teaming up; this was literally what they were designed to do.

After the Boly handball, former referee Dermot Gallagher praised the system and said it was working as intended:

> It [the Boly handball] was only controversial as people were not aware the law had changed. It was correct – the referee has no choice. The law changed in the summer and if a player is struck on the arm or hand by the ball and it goes into the net then the goal will be disallowed. It is a mandatory thing, there's no grey area.[1]

But while Gallagher was adamant the new system was working well, many other people were not so sure. It felt incredibly harsh to rule out goals as a result of the ball accidentally brushing players on the hand. In reference to the Laporte incident, the *Match of the Day* pundit Danny Murphy said, 'The new handball rule is ridiculous. That should never on any playing field anywhere in the world be disallowed.' He also emphasised the link between the new law and VAR: 'It wouldn't even be seen if we didn't have VAR.' His fellow pundit Alan Shearer said, 'There is not one player on that pitch who thought that was a handball or who complained.'

But it was not an isolated incident. Similar examples piled up as the season went on. In January 2020, West

Ham had a last-minute equaliser against Sheffield United ruled out for a handball. The goal was scored by Robert Snodgrass, but Declan Rice was penalised for an accidental handball in the build-up to the goal. Again, this infringement would not have been spotted without VAR, and even if it had been, under the previous law it would have been deemed accidental. In this case, it felt particularly harsh because quite a few seconds elapsed between the handball and the goal. After the ball brushed his hand, Rice shook off one opponent, dribbled past two others and passed to Snodgrass, who scored. We all thought that the point of the law change was to prevent incidents where the ball deflects off someone's hand into the goal. Instead, it is picking up incredibly marginal accidental handballs that occur at the very start of a chain of events that lead to a goal.

After this match, the former referee Chris Foy wrote an article for the Premier League website, saying that overturning the goal 'was the correct decision and good use of VAR'. But he also said that he understood Rice's frustration and that the decision was right according 'to the letter of the law'. His phrasing made it clear that there was something about the decision that was *not* right according to the spirit of the law.

The response of IFAB wasn't to go back to the old discretionary law, but to further refine the new one. It was changed again for the start of the 2020–21 season, in a way that was specifically designed to address incidents like the Rice handball. The 2020–21 law said that an accidental handball must happen 'immediately' before a goal or goal-scoring opportunity to count as an infringement. It will not be an offence 'if the ball travels some distance via a pass or a dribble, or there are several passes before the goal or goalscoring opportunity'. In theory, this meant Rice's handball would not have been an infringement under the new law, and Snodgrass's goal would have stood.

But the controversies kept on coming. In a game against Tottenham in September 2020, the Newcastle striker Andy Carroll headed the ball onto the Spurs defender Eric Dier's arm. Dier's back was turned to Carroll and he could not even see the ball, but after a VAR check, the referee awarded a penalty. Steve Bruce, the Newcastle manager who benefited from the decision, said, 'If you're going to tell me that is handball, then we all may as well pack it in. It's a nonsense, a nonsense of a rule. It's gone for us today – however, it's ludicrous.'

We are used to managers criticising referees when decisions go against them, but never before had I heard a manager who benefited from one criticise it so severely. When that happens, you know the system isn't working. The *Guardian*'s match report said, 'This was perhaps the worst among a long list of maddening recent decisions brought about by a rule that goes against the sport's very essence.' It was essentially a more formal way of saying what fans had been chanting in grounds for months: it's not football any more.

Even though it was only September and the new law had

been in operation in the Premier League for barely two months, the outcry forced a change. In England, a group called the Professional Game Match Officials Limited (PGMOL) is responsible for the refereeing of games. At the start of the 2020–21 season, it had instructed referees in England to follow the new IFAB law exactly. But after the Dier handball and others like it, they asked them to be more lenient in their interpretation.

TECHNOLOGY GIVES, AND TECHNOLOGY TAKES AWAY

By this point, VAR and the new handball law didn't just feel like a tweak to the game's laws, but a massive rent in its fabric. I kept wondering: what would happen if you went back and refereed old matches according to this new law and with this new technology? How many previously uncontroversial goals would you end up ruling out?

The saga rolled on throughout the 2019–20 and 2020–21 seasons, at the same time as the Covid pandemic forced most professional leagues to stop. The 2019–20 Premier League season was paused in March and resumed behind closed doors in June. The 2020–21 season was mostly played in empty stadiums. Those eerie lockdown matches emphasised football's reliance on technology. Those of us with season tickets at Premier League clubs had known deep down for years that we were pretty irrelevant in the grand scheme of football finances, but the lockdown matches brought home just how insignificant we were. Players could keep drawing their vast salaries as long as the TV audiences were watching, and as long as the money from global TV rights kept rolling in.

But the same slow-motion video replays and camera angles that had helped export the Premier League around the world were now revealing things about the reality of football that undermined its foundations. Handballs seemed to be everywhere. Offsides were more common than we thought. Nothing was clear and obvious.

It reminded me of the history of Christianity. Protestant-ism had flourished in the 16th and 17th centuries thanks to the invention of the printing press, which could spread the word of God and new ideas about faith to new audiences. But it hit a crisis in the 18th and 19th centuries as the next generations of Protestant reformers used technology to closely examine the Bible, the life of Christ and the history of the Earth itself. What they discovered undermined a lot of people's assumptions, and caused a lot of confusion too. New insights made it harder for the everyday person to understand and engage with faith. More conservative Protestants worried about the effect of all this research. If you over-complicate things, maybe you will just scare people off religion entirely and turn them into atheists. Maybe you'll drive them into the arms of religions that can offer more certainty. Nobody wants that.

Early on in the handball saga, Rio Ferdinand made a similar point:

> If you add too much to this game you are going to detach it from the everyday man or woman coming in to the game. Look at American sports – a lot of people outside America wouldn't watch it because they think there's too much going on and too many rules. That's the beauty of our game – it's simple, everyone can play it. That's starting to change now and I hope it doesn't go too far.[2]

If you keep messing about with the traditional structures of the game, people might get turned off and stop following the sport. Or, God forbid, they might start following American football instead.

Nobody wants that.

Ferdinand is right that simplicity matters. The deeper subtext of his comment is also quite radical, and surprising for an ex-professional footballer. For years we have heard players say that they just want referees to get decisions right; that if they need help from technology, we should bring it in; that footballers' and managers' livelihoods depend on the right decision.

But what Ferdinand is suggesting here is that getting the right decisions isn't everything. Other things matter too, and having a game that flows smoothly and is simple for everyone to understand is also important. In a more fundamental way, the livelihood of every player and manager depends on football being a sport that fans want to watch. There are limits to our desire for the right decisions.

THE WORST OF BOTH WORLDS

Consistency and common sense are in tension. A law that allows for the application of common sense will probably not be consistent, and one that maximises consistency will probably not allow for common sense. Football's authorities are aware of this. David Elleray is a former Premier League referee and the current technical director of IFAB. He's been responsible for many of IFAB's law changes over the past few years and has said that 'the challenge is that some people want more and more detail, because they want 100 per cent consistency, other people want more flexibility, i.e. common sense. And as you know, you can't have both consistency and common sense because handball is subjective.'[3]

However, the awkward effect of the new laws is that we have sacrificed a lot of common sense without actually gaining the hoped-for consistency. We have ended up with the worst of both worlds: reduced common sense and reduced consistency. That's because the laws have been drawn up tightly enough to prevent discretion, but not tightly enough to provide consistency.

For example, the day after the Declan Rice handball, some West Ham players posted pictures of handballs that had led to goals and *not* been penalised. In one particularly striking example from just a couple of months before, the ball had hit the outstretched arm of Liverpool's Trent Alexander-Arnold in his own penalty box. No penalty was awarded. Liverpool immediately went up the other end and scored, but the goal was not disallowed. This handball felt far more significant, obvious and deliberate than Rice's, but it did not result in an infringement. This was exactly the kind of inconsistency that the new law was supposed to prevent. But it hasn't, because while it is strict about what it defines as a handball, it is not so strict about what it defines as 'creating a goal-scoring opportunity'. In this example, the officials made a judgement that Alexander-Arnold's handball did not create a goal-scoring opportunity.

The law change after the Rice handball theoretically meant that such cases would no longer be an infringement. However, there is enough ambiguity in the way the new law is phrased for different referees to make different judgements. The law was changed to say it is an offence 'if a player, after the ball has touched their or a team-mate's hand/arm, even if accidental, immediately creates a goal-scoring opportunity'. It is not an offence 'if, after an accidental handball, the ball travels some distance (pass or dribble) and/or there are several passes before the goal or goal-scoring opportunity'. What does 'immediately' mean? What does 'some distance' mean? How many passes is 'several'?

We are still in worst-of-both-worlds territory: we've removed enough discretion to permit absurdities, but not enough to eliminate inconsistencies.

Frequent law changes create a further type of inconsistency, as Kevin de Bruyne has noticed. In November 2020, after another confusing VAR handball decision that depended on another tweak to the laws, the Manchester City forward summed up the problems caused by the constant chopping and changing:

> I don't know the rules anymore, honestly. I thought if it was above the arm here, then it's not handball anymore, but the law changes. Now it's the middle of the arm. Everybody knows it hits him but honestly, I don't know the rules.
>
> If you listen tomorrow, the day after, it will come on whatever channel and the referee will say it's a good decision so it really doesn't matter.
>
> What can we say? I have been playing professional football for 12 years and in the first nine years, there were no rule changes. Then in the last three years, there has been a lot of rule changes.
>
> I don't know why. Football is such a nice game. The guys who make the rules should be people in the game.

I don't know who makes them. I would just say, be consistent, that's it. The strict handball law was brought in to create more consistency. It has failed to do that, and it has also created a new form of inconsistency, as it is constantly being adjusted mid-season. It is also interpreted in different ways in different competitions.

While the laws of the game are set by IFAB, different authorities can issue guidance and advice on exactly how they are interpreted. PGMOL, which manages Premier League referees, seems to allow a bit more latitude and discretion than UEFA, which manages those in the Champions League. But it's not always exactly clear what the guidance is, and if it is permitted by IFAB.

In the 2023–24 season, Paris Saint-Germain were awarded a late penalty in their Champions League group stage match against Newcastle, after the referee reviewed his initial decision and decided Tino Livramento had in fact handled the ball. The decision was both controversial and confusing. The replay showed the ball bounced off Livramento's chest and onto his arm. According to the *Guardian*, which analysed the decision, there was some confusion about UEFA's guidance on incidents where the ball bounces off a body part and onto the arm.

Rio Ferdinand pointed out the problems with over-complicating the sport for fans, but the constant law changes and updates are also over-complicating the sport for referees. The handball law is now exceptionally hard to understand and apply. Five years of constant tinkering has resulted in confusion and inconsistency. The attempt to define in prose every possible combination of circumstances in which a ball might hit a hand has not worked. As we will see in Chapter 7, words are not capable of performing this task.

MAXIMISING CONSISTENCY

We are in a situation where we have traded off the referee's discretion in search of greater consistency, but have ended up with neither. Suppose we did want to achieve greater consistency and didn't care about what was lost in its pursuit. What should we do?

If you want to prioritise consistency above all else, you should eliminate the judgement of the referee and the detailed rule book. You should change the law so that *all* handballs are infringements, wherever and whenever they occur. You should then kit out the ball and the outfield players' hands and arms with sensors that sound automatically as soon as the ball touches them. This would provide you with consistency, but it would also transform the game. Wingers would have dedicated training sessions where they would practise hitting the ball against the arms of defenders. Defenders would practise running and jumping with their hands behind their backs. The game would be much less like the one we are used to. It really would not be football any more.

This seems too absurd to be possible, but recent developments suggest maybe it is not so far-fetched. Euro 2024 saw the debut of the 'snickometer', a sensor in the ball that detects handball infringements. It felt like a triumph of technological capability over common sense, a technological solution in search of a problem. In cricket, where the snickometer works well, knowing whether a ball has hit the bat or not is useful and largely conclusive. But in football, the problems with the handball law are not being caused by uncertainty about whether players touched the ball or not; they are being caused by uncertainty about what types of handball should count as infringements. The snickometer can't solve that problem.

WAS FOOTBALL CREATED FOR VAR?

The tension between the spirit and the letter of the law is not new or unique to football; in fact, it goes back to the foundation of Christianity. In the Gospel of Mark, Jesus and his disciples pick some heads of grain on the Sabbath. The Pharisees criticise them for breaking the rule about not working on the day of rest. Jesus tells them that the Sabbath was made for man, not man for the Sabbath.

I think of this whenever I hear people complain about VAR. Was football created for VAR, or was VAR created for football?

If you were an early Christian critiquing the Pharisees, you would say: build a religion on your principles, and you will end up with a lot of rule-followers who miss the bigger picture. If you were a Pharisee critiquing the Christians, you would say: build a religion on your principles, and it won't *be* a religion because it will descend into self-serving, anarchic in-fighting over the meaning of 'the spirit'.

Shakespeare was fond of dramatising debates about the letter and the spirit of the law. In *Henry VI: Part 2*, a character called Dick the Butcher is part of a popular rebellion against the government. He gathers with his comrades on Blackheath ahead of their march on London and tells them, 'The first thing we do, let's kill all the lawyers.' If you were a lawyer criticising the rebels, you would say: this is what mobs do – they break rules and create chaos and anarchy. If you were defending the rebels, you would argue that they represent a higher justice.

People like Dick the Butcher would say that the problem with lawyers is the way they manipulate the law so that they are always on the right side of it. At the end of the 2019–20 season, the Premier League released data showing that the previous season, referees got 82% of decisions right, but now, with VAR, they were getting 94% correct. That sounds impressive, until you realise that the 94%

included a lot of controversial disallowed goals where most people didn't even realise there was a handball.

Indeed, if you wanted to be cynical, you could wonder why VAR isn't achieving a 100% success rate, given that the laws of the game have been rewritten to suit it. A Dick the Butcher critique of VAR would say that the real job of football's authorities is to create and enforce laws that make sense to both fans and players. They are not capable of that, however, so they use their power to change the laws to make their lives easier and make it look like they are being successful. And then they patronise anyone who is unhappy with the result by telling them that they don't understand the laws and statistics.

Football fans' unhappiness with VAR is best reflected in the chant that's become common after controversial VAR decisions: 'It's not football any more.' This chant is a great summary of the argument for following the spirit of the law. If you enforce the laws according to the letter, then perhaps football will be clearer to understand, easier to administer and more logically defensible. But it will not be football. Perhaps we may not be able to explain in words exactly what football is, but we know it when we see it, and this isn't it.

The same tensions between the spirit and the letter of the law exist in other areas. Over the last few decades, exam boards have faced many of the same dilemmas as football's lawmakers. You can apply a spirit-of-the-law approach to assessment, whereby a marker has a lot of discretion and can use their common sense. But this will result in inconsistencies: two students can submit similar responses and get different marks.

Many exam boards have moved to more of a letter-of-the-law approach, where the marker has more guidance from a mark scheme and less discretion. The problem with this is similar to the one with the new handball law: essays that don't conform precisely to the requirements of the marking scheme do not get a good grade, even if they are brilliant. Others that are not as good get a better grade because they tick the boxes on the mark scheme.

There is also a further problem, which has been labelled with a bit of assessment jargon: 'negative washback'. This is when your rule changes start to affect the way the subject is taught. In England, primary pupils' writing is assessed against a fairly strict letter-of-the-law-style mark scheme, part of which requires the use of adverbials. So pupils are now taught to use them, but will often do so in ways that don't make sense, like 'Forgettably, he crept through the darkness.'

The football equivalent is the full-back who runs with their hands behind their back to try and prevent any contact with the ball. Inflexible applications of rules almost always lead to these kinds of distortions.

IS IMPROVEMENT POSSIBLE?

We want common sense and consistency. There are four possible combinations of these two variables:

- High common sense, low consistency. This is the spirit-of-the-law approach. It keeps the laws relatively broadly defined and relies on the on-field referee to apply them. This is the traditional model of refereeing. It will result in a recognisable game of football, but it will also lead to a lot of inconsistencies.
- Low common sense, high consistency. This is the letter-of-the-law approach, where you remove human judgement entirely. This would happen if we introduced snickometer-style sensor systems that automatically flag an infringement. It would eliminate inconsistency, but only by dramatically changing the way the game works.
- Low common sense, low consistency. This is what we have at the moment, and is the worst of both worlds: referees have limited discretion to overturn decisions like the Rice and Dier handballs, but ambiguity – and, therefore, inconsistency – still exists.
- High common sense, high consistency.

This is the combination we all want, a method of refereeing that eliminates inconsistency but still allows us to enjoy what we recognise as football. Is this even possible?

Low consistency It's football!	High consistency It's football!
• Traditional 'spirit of the law' refereeing • Referee has discretion • Lots of inconsistency	• Is this possible?
Low consistency It's not football any more	High consistency It's not football any more
• VAR • Sacrifices meaning and discretion in order to improve consistency – but fails to achieve that, too • The worst of both worlds	• Sensor-based handball monitoring • Ball and players are kitted out with sensors, and a buzzer sounds whenever the ball touches a player's arm or hand.

Perhaps not. The structure of football is in some ways in opposition to consistency. The things that we love about the game and that make it what it is – its speed, its fluidity, its unpredictability, its simplicity – are all qualities that make consistency harder, or perhaps even impossible, to achieve. Inconsistency may well be a feature of football, not a bug.

As a result, if we want football to remain recognisably 'football', I don't think it is possible to achieve perfect consistency. However, I do think there are ways of increasing consistency that would not dramatically alter the nature of the game, and in Part 2 I will outline them in more detail. I believe this is possible because these same tensions between common sense and consistency exist in many other fields, and they have found more effective ways to resolve them, using technologies that are currently not being used in football.

But before we get there, I want to consider another possible solution: to give up on the goal of consistency. Accept that inconsistency is the price you pay for the game being the way it is. Use technology, not to eliminate inconsistency, but for the more modest goal of correcting glaring errors. After all, as we saw in the Introduction, that was the real motivation behind the adoption of video technology. We can probably live with a bit of inconsistency; what we really need to care about, and what really brings the game into disrepute, are obvious errors like the Thierry Henry handball. That should be a much simpler problem to solve.

And the guidance on the use of VAR recognises this point. It distinguishes between what it calls 'factual' and 'subjective' decisions. Factual decisions are those that have been defined precisely by the letter of the law. But the guidance acknowledges that some decisions, like judging whether a tackle is a foul or not, are not like this, and instead depend on the discretion of the on-field referee. These subjective decisions should be overturned by VAR only if the on-field referee has made a 'clear and obvious error'. Given how difficult it is to achieve perfect consistency, surely this is quite a sensible approach? In the next chapter, we will see how it is working out.

2

FOULS

'If you give me six lines written by the hand of the most
honest of men, I will find something in them which will
hang him.'

Cardinal Richelieu

WHAT IS 'CLEAR AND OBVIOUS'?

Subjective decisions, like judgements about the severity of
a foul, should be overturned only if the original decision
was a 'clear and obvious error'. What is a 'clear and obvious
error'? Chris Foy, a former referee who was involved in the
implementation of VAR, explained that it is the kind of
incident 'where everyone goes "crikey".'

The theory behind setting a high bar for the review of
subjective decisions was that nobody wanted every game

being re-refereed from a video room. There will always be decisions you can argue about, but the 'clear and obvious' bar was designed to ensure that VAR would be used sparingly to overturn obviously bad decisions.

That is not what has happened.

Soon after VAR is introduced it becomes clear and obvious that nobody has a clue what 'clear and obvious' means.

In one early controversy, the Arsenal defender Sokratis thinks he has scored a late winner against Crystal Palace, but the video assistant referee reviews the decision and decides the on-field referee has missed a foul in the build-up to the goal. When you watch the replay, you can definitely see that there might have been a foul. But is it a clear and obvious error? Is it the kind of incident where everyone goes, 'Crikey'?

This is what people end up debating. 'I can see how that *might* have been a foul/penalty/red card,' they will say. 'But was the original decision really a clear and obvious error?'

It is true that decisions about fouls and red cards are subjective and discretionary. But whether something is a clear and obvious error is equally subjective and discretionary. So all that VAR has done is added another layer of subjectivity. It hasn't reduced controversy; it's doubled it. Now, you can argue not only about whether a challenge truly was reckless, but also whether it was reckless enough to be a clear and obvious error.

The guidance soon gets tweaked to give the on-field

referee a bit more control over decisions. The VAR can ask the referee to review their decision using a screen at the side of the pitch. You might think that referees would be less likely to want to blame themselves for a clear and obvious error, but that's not the case. Once they are called to the pitchside monitor, they generally tend to overturn their original decisions, even ones that most observers don't think are clear and obvious errors.

In fact, there are plenty of high-profile cases of referees making a decision, reviewing it on the pitchside monitor and deciding to overturn it because it is a clear and obvious error, and then having that decision overturned in the next few days by an FA appeal panel. In February 2021, there are two such incidents within a few days, both involving the same referee. First, Mike Dean sends off the Southampton defender Jan Bednarek after reviewing the incident on a pitchside monitor. The decision is overturned after the match by an FA appeal panel. A few days later, Dean sends off the West Ham player Tomáš Souček after a pitchside monitor review in a match against Fulham. Again, the decision is overturned afterwards on appeal. Theoretically, the ability a referee has to review and overturn their decisions mid-match should have reduced or even eliminated the need to have post-match appeals. Instead, it's given the appeal panels another type of error to deal with. We are in a hall of mirrors: referees are making errors in their judgement of what an error is.

In 2024, there's a high-profile disagreement about the meaning of 'clear and obvious' in the Euro 2024 semi-final between England and the Netherlands. A loose ball breaks to Harry Kane in the penalty area, and he hits a shot on goal on the half-volley. The Netherlands defender Denzil Dumfries charges across to block the shot and crashes into Kane after he gets the shot away. Kane goes down hurt, but there is no real appeal for a penalty from him or any of the England players.

What is particularly interesting about what happens next is that the decision-making process is commented on live by ITV's refereeing expert, Christina Unkel. At every stage, what she says should happen does not. First, the commentators ask her if VAR will review the decision. She says, 'No, no suggestion from the VAR for a recommendation for a penalty . . . It should be a check and release.' Almost as soon as she finishes saying these words, the exact opposite happens: the VAR requests that the referee reviews his decision on the pitchside monitor. Unkel is confused: 'I am quite surprised that this is being sent [for review], and in fact the preferred recommendation is for this not to be a penalty.'

Everybody at home knows exactly what is coming next. Almost as soon as she has said 'not to be a penalty', the on-field referee signals a penalty. The most perceptive analysis of the situation comes not from Unkel, but from Ally McCoist, who is co-commentating on the match. 'The fact [the referee's] running over – sorry, Christina, I'll be astonished if he doesn't give it.' McCoist knows that once a referee is called to the pitchside monitor, they are likely to overturn their original decision.

It was the perfect example of why 'clear and obvious' isn't clear and obvious. If qualified referees can disagree that profoundly about what a 'clear and obvious' error is, how can anything about the decision be said to be clear or obvious?

In the media the next day, Unkel doubled down on her interpretation, explaining exactly why the incident was not a penalty and why the original decision should not have been reviewed. I was inclined to agree with her analysis of the incident. But I did not agree at all with the implication of her argument, which was essentially to defend the VAR system and blame the individual referee. Similar incidents have happened repeatedly now over a period of six years, and when that happens you cannot keep blaming the individual; you have to look at the system.

The pitchside monitor judgements about what is 'clear and obvious' are just as subjective and inconsistent as on-field judgements about what a penalty is and what a red card is. Unkel's passive-voice phrasing – 'the preferred recommendation is for this not to be a penalty' – provides a veneer of objectivity and impersonality to a system that is highly unreliable and inconsistent.

THE SLOW-MOTION REPLAY

Why are the pitchside monitor reviews so problematic? It may have something to do with the effect of slow-motion replays.

In a match between Brighton and Liverpool, shortly after the introduction of pitchside monitor reviews, Brighton are awarded a penalty after the on-field referee overturns his initial decision. The Liverpool full-back Andy Robertson had cleared the ball, but in doing so had also hit the foot of Brighton's Danny Welbeck.

In the following day's papers, two ex-referees provided different opinions on the decision. Chris Foy defended it, arguing that it was 'a wild kick' by Robertson that caught Welbeck, while Dermot Gallagher disagreed, saying, 'It's a really harsh call.' But both men highlighted the role of the slow-motion replay. Foy said that it let you see that the kick was wild, while Gallagher claimed that it distorted reality. 'When you look at it in slow motion,' he said, 'it's a penalty, there's an anomaly between the referee and VAR – when you see it at full speed it's a different incident.'[4]

The impact of slow-motion replays has been studied by researchers in a different context. In a 2009 murder trial in the US, prosecution lawyers slowed down footage of the defendant shooting a police officer, to show that the act was premeditated and therefore deserved the charge of first-degree murder. The defence argued that slowing the footage down like that created 'a false impression of premeditation', and that the defendant was guilty instead of second-degree murder.

A group of researchers decided to investigate the issue further, carrying out a series of experiments using surveillance footage of actual murders and replays of violent contact in American football matches.[5] They showed that people do perceive an action as more intentional when they see it in a slow-motion replay, compared with real time.

Another group of investigators took a similar approach, but instead used fouls from soccer matches and asked elite referees to judge them. The effect persisted: the referees made harsher decisions when they viewed the infringements in slow motion rather than in real time.[6]

Who is right here? Are slow-motion replays giving a more accurate insight into reality? Is the increased perception of intentionality correct, and are the harsher punishments justified? Or are these delusions caused by the slowing-down? Are our real-time perceptions more accurate because they take place in real time, or less so because it is so easy to miss things?

Whatever your response to these questions, one thing is undeniable: if you change your decision-making process from one that is based on real-time perception to one reliant on slow-motion replays, you will get different decisions. You can argue over whether one process is more or less accurate than the other; what you can't argue is that the two processes are equivalent. They will result in different outcomes. You may think that Robertson's foul deserves a penalty, but you have to acknowledge that without a slow-motion replay, it is highly unlikely any referee would award one.

The authorities seem to be aware of this, and in the latest protocols for VAR they say that slow-motion replays should be used only to establish 'facts', which include things like 'position of offence/player, point of contact for physical offences and handball, ball out of play (including goal/no goal)'.

Normal speed should be used for more subjective decisions, such as 'the "intensity" of an offence or to decide if it was a handball offence'.

But this is a difficult distinction to make. The same incident might involve a 'factual' decision and a 'subjective' one: for example, a referee might first of all need to see if a foul has taken place in the penalty area or not, which is a factual decision, so a slow-motion replay is allowed. But then they have to decide if a foul has taken place, for which slow-motion replays should not be used. To what extent can they simply 'forget' the slow-motion replay they've seen? A game that allows referees to view slow-motion replays is going to end up with different decisions to one that doesn't have them.

FACTUAL OR SUBJECTIVE?

More broadly, dividing decisions into categories of 'factual' and 'subjective' causes other problems. We saw at the start of the chapter that factual decisions are not subject to the 'clear and obvious' threshold that subjective ones are. This means that they can be overturned, even if they are very marginal, whereas a subjective decision must clear a higher bar.

But as we've just seen, individual incidents can often involve two different decisions, one of which is subjective and one which isn't. Handballs are a combination of factual decisions about whether the ball hit the hand and subjective decisions about whether the handball immediately led to a goal-scoring opportunity. The factual/subjective distinction is one of the most confusing aspects of VAR, and often you will hear fans applying the 'clear and obvious' test to a factual decision, where it is not meant to be used.

The 'clear and obvious' test doesn't apply to factual decisions, because they are supposed to have a definitive right answer that can be established by technology. In theory, this should make them relatively straightforward, without any of the confusion surrounding subjective decisions. But as we will see in the next chapter, they have proved to be far more complicated than anyone could have imagined.

3

LINE CALLS

'Football is a simple game made complicated by people who should know better.'

Bill Shankly

THE LIMITS OF HUMAN CAPACITY

In the 2010 World Cup, there were two bad refereeing errors on the same day. First, Frank Lampard scored what became known as a 'ghost goal' for England against Germany, after his shot bounced down off the crossbar and back into the field of play. The referee decided it hadn't crossed the goal line, but replays showed that it was at least a foot over. Had the goal been awarded, the score would have been 2–2. Germany went on to win the match 4–1.

A few hours later, Carlos Tevez scored the opening goal for Argentina against Mexico, despite being in a clear off-side position. In this case, replays of the goal were shown by accident on the big screen in the stadium moments later. The entire crowd could see that Tevez had been offside, but there was nothing the referee could do to change his decision.

As with the Thierry Henry handball, these two incidents brought renewed calls for technology to be introduced to help referees. Goal-line decisions and offsides are both line calls, where the official has to decide whether the ball or a player is over a certain line or not. They are straightforward yes/no decisions that are nevertheless exceptionally hard for humans to make in real time because they strain the limits of our capacity. Referees and their assistants will often be a few dozen metres away from the goal line and at an unhelpful angle. Offside is even harder: the assistant referee has to monitor at least three players at exactly the same time – the player kicking the ball, the one receiving it and the penultimate defender.

Equivalent line decisions in other sports already use technology. In cricket, run-outs have been subject to video review since 1992. Since 2006, many major tennis tournaments have used computer-vision technology to allow players to challenge line calls. And in 2013, similar technology was introduced in the Premier League to help determine whether shots had crossed the goal line. By and large, it has been successful, although there have been a couple of notable errors. In June 2020, Sheffield United should have been awarded a goal against Aston Villa, after the Villa keeper carried a free kick over the line. The system missed it because all seven of its cameras were blocked by either defenders, the goalkeeper or the goalposts. In September 2022, Huddersfield were denied a goal in a Championship match against Blackpool, again because the cameras' views were blocked. Still, despite these errors, goal-line technology (GLT) mostly works well, and most fans are supportive of it.

The success of GLT reassured people that technology in football could work and paved the way for its greater use. If it could work so well with goal-line decisions, it seemed reasonable to assume that it would work well with offsides, too. These are more complicated than goal-line decisions, and as we will see, they do have some subjective elements. But most of them involve a line call about whether a player is ahead of the penultimate defender at the moment the ball is played.

It felt as though technology would provide an ideal solution to judging offside, but that is not what has happened at all. Perhaps the most surprising aspect of VAR is that its offside decisions are probably the most controversial of all, more so even than the far more subjective penalty and handball decisions, and certainly far more than GLT.

ARMPIT OFFSIDES

The first VAR offside controversy in the Premier League came in the first weekend it was used: West Ham vs Manchester City in August 2019. I was at this match, but as is typically the case with VAR, it was only when I got home later and watched the highlights that I realised what had happened. City had played a fast passing move, with David Silva flicking the ball on to Raheem Sterling, who then squared it for Gabriel Jesus to score. However, the VAR review showed that when Silva played his pass, Sterling was 2.4 centimetres offside, and the goal was disallowed.

This incident did cause some comment, but as City won 5–0 anyway, it was not really that significant. However, over the following few months there was a succession of similar decisions at more crucial moments in matches, which therefore generated more debate.

Perhaps the peak moment of controversy happened a couple of months later, in November 2019, when Liverpool's Roberto Firmino had a goal disallowed for offside against Aston Villa. Firmino was judged to be offside by the on-field officials, and the decision was reviewed by VAR. On the slow-motion replay and the still image taken at the moment the ball was played, Firmino looked as though he was onside. His body seemed to be behind the penultimate defender. But VAR disagreed and said he was off.

At half-time, the Premier League decided to post an update on their Twitter account explaining the decision. They posted the still image of Firmino at the moment the ball was played, with a red offside line superimposed on top of it. Their explanation was as follows: 'The red line signifies Firmino and was aligned to his armpit, which was marginally ahead of the last Villa defender.'

If they had hoped this would clear up the matter, they were wrong. It just aggravated people even more. In fact, the concept of the 'armpit offside' became a shorthand for all that was wrong with VAR: its pettiness, its pedantry, its attempt to shoehorn the fluidity and volatility of football into categories that were entirely inappropriate.

In December 2019, after three armpit offsides in one day, players and ex-players queued up to criticise the system. Gary Lineker said that 'if you have to draw lines and dots and it's still not clear one way or the other, then please stop undermining the on-field officials. Absurd.'[7] Jermaine Jenas said that 'Fans are not enjoying what's happening, players are not celebrating. I really hope IFAB are not stubborn enough to realise something needs to change to stop that occurring. For offsides I'd get rid of it.'[8]

The former England manager Roy Hodgson took on the role of the wise Cassandra figure, pointing out that fans had demanded this and really had only themselves to blame. 'I was never one to be banging the drum for VAR, but if the mass media want it, and the public want it once again you have to be mature enough to accept it. I'm one of the ones sensible enough, or logical enough to accept that we wanted it, we've got it, it's there for us so we get on with it.'[9]

The offside heels and toes carried on piling up throughout

that first season, and in November 2020 came perhaps the most absurd VAR offside of all, when the Leeds striker Patrick Bamford's upper arm was deemed offside, after he used it to point out to a teammate exactly where he wanted the ball.

At the end of the 2023–24 season, the complaints were still there. In April 2024, one of the most dramatic FA Cup matches in history ended with a VAR offside controversy. Manchester United were 3–0 up against Coventry City with 20 minutes to go, but Coventry scored three late goals to take the tie into extra time. Near the end of the additional thirty minutes, Coventry's Victor Torp scored after a well-worked move.

The Coventry fans and players erupted in delight at one of the greatest comebacks ever. Except it wasn't. The VAR deemed that in the build-up to the goal, Haji Wright had been marginally offside. It was another occasion where the still images showed the incident to be incredibly tight, and the judgement felt unbelievably harsh. That decision dominated the coverage of the match, and even after United went on to win the Cup by beating Manchester City in the final, it was still being discussed and debated.

The offside law is far clearer than the laws about handball and other fouls, and far harder for a human to apply. It feels like the kind of problem technology could easily solve. How on earth has it caused so much controversy?

THE MEASUREMENT TECHNOLOGY IS NOT
ACCURATE ENOUGH

If the VAR system is making decisions about armpits, toes and heels being offside, then we need to have confidence that the technology is capable of such precision. Let's go back to the very first VAR offside in the Premier League, when Raheem Sterling was judged to be the victim, and see how the system works.

To decide if he is offside, the VAR has to freeze the video replay at the moment the ball was played to Sterling. This is when David Silva's boot first touches the ball.

However, the camera used by VAR takes 50 frames per second – that is, one frame every 0.02 seconds. The referee has to pause the footage on the first frame that shows Silva's boot hitting the ball, but in reality, this might have happened somewhere in between two frames.

Sterling is rapid. His top speed is just over 30 kph. He wasn't going this fast for this 'goal', though; let's say he was going at just 15 kph. That's about 4 metres per second, which is about 8 centimetres every 0.02 seconds. So in our 0.02 seconds of uncertainty, where we are not sure if Silva has touched the ball or not, Sterling has moved about 8 centimetres. And yet he was deemed by VAR to have been offside by 2.4 centimetres.

Hypothetically, this situation could be even worse. Imagine a situation where an extremely quick defender and attacker are both moving at top speed in opposite directions. In this case, in our 0.02-second window of uncertainty the defender is moving about 16 centimetres in one direction and the attacker 16 centimetres in the other.

Once the footage has been frozen at the first frame where the ball is played, the video assistant referee must then decide where to draw the offside lines and where to place crosshairs indicating the relevant defender and attacker. This is another potential source of error, as different referees could disagree on where to place those lines and crosshairs.

You could work out the extent of this error by having a hundred different video referees independently judge the same offside decision. If they all placed the lines and crosshairs in the same place, you could conclude that the error from this source was not significant. As far as I know, no research measuring this type of error has been published. But such mistakes definitely exist, because as we will see in Chapter 5, there are examples of referees drawing the lines and crosshairs on the wrong players.

These are important points, and they are worth thinking about. But are they actually the source of our angst about VAR offsides?

No measurement on Earth is completely accurate. They all contain some error. VAR was introduced because the mistakes made by humans using the naked eye were much greater than ±8 centimetres. Back in the 2013–14 season, when Sterling was playing for Liverpool *against* Manchester City, he had a goal ruled out for offside, despite replays showing he was very clearly onside. VAR offside judgements do have some measurement error. Human offside judgements have more. Suppose we had some way of using technology to further reduce or even eliminate this measurement error. Would that reduce the outrage these decisions have caused? Suppose after the Coventry City offside someone had said, 'Hold on, let's ring up CERN and see if they've got any physicists who can help us out here.' And suppose the physicists had taken a few minutes to ping some photons around Wembley and concluded that yes, Wright *was* offside, and they could locate the precise cells in his toe that had transgressed. Would we have been happy then? No, of course not. We'd have gone even crazier.

The problem isn't that VAR is inaccurate. It is that it is too accurate. We are back to the same problem we had with handball and penalties: VAR is *more* accurate than the previous system, and its accuracy is revealing things about reality that we don't like.

The offside law wasn't written with frame rates in mind. Before VAR, it was about whether a player was ahead of or level with the penultimate defender. The law didn't bother defining the specific part of a player that needed to be ahead of or level with the penultimate defender, because no human would be capable of making a decision that precise in real time.

As we've seen, offside is difficult for humans to judge because it tests the limits of our perception. But precisely because it is so difficult for us to assess, it has probably *never* been implemented accurately. Some of the offside toes, heels and armpits would simply never have been spotted in the past. Some phases of play just wouldn't have been scrutinised as much. And it isn't only referees who have been missing these offsides, but everyone else too.

According to the letter of the law, heels and armpits can be offside. But it doesn't *feel* like offside. Roy Hodgson summed up this point of view after Crystal Palace were denied a goal because of a tight offside call: 'We get the situation where people are becoming a bit disillusioned because they're seeing good goals chalked off by very small margins of space, if you like.' Hodgson was right to say that people were getting disillusioned by these decisions, and I agree with him that some of these decisions do just feel wrong.

But what's interesting is that we don't have the same reaction to close goal-line decisions. When we see a beautiful bit of skill lead to a shot that bounces down off the crossbar and lands just the wrong side of the goal line, we might bemoan a team's misfortune, but we don't complain that 'good goals are being chalked off by very small margins of space'. Nor do we demand that the laws of the game be rewritten to provide for thinner goal lines. We just accept that that's the way it is.

But when it comes to offside, it feels like these marginal decisions are infringing some fundamental spirit of the law. Why does offside exist, and what is it designed to achieve?

THE SPIRIT OF THE OFFSIDE LAW

The aim of the offside law is to stop goal-hanging and encourage shorter passing and dribbling. If it didn't exist, then there would be nothing to stop players surrounding the goalkeeper, with their team's defenders pumping long balls up to them.

But creating a law that stops goal-hanging is much harder than it seems. You can't completely ban players from going near the opposition goal. You only want to stop them from surrounding the goalkeeper in certain circumstances.

The first offside law, introduced in 1863, stipulated that a player was offside if he was ahead of the ball. This certainly promoted dribbling, albeit at the expense of both short and long passes. In 1866, the law was amended so that a player was onside if he was behind at least three defensive players at the moment the ball was played. In 1925, it was changed again to two defenders, the number that we are used to today.

You could argue that all of these variants of the offside law were too strict. They certainly prevented goal-hanging, and they also stopped play being stretched over large spaces.

But they arguably went too far in the other direction. Play ended up compressed inside a narrow band either side of the halfway line, and defensive teams employed stifling offside traps, which was never the law's intention.

After the 1990 World Cup, the law was changed, so that an attacking player did not have to be behind the penultimate defender to be onside, but only level. Since then there have been a handful of arcane but important adjustments to the law, all of which have been in the attacker's favour, and all designed to encourage attacking football. The most important of these changes came in 2005, when the definition of 'being involved in active play' was clarified in a way that benefited the attacking team.It is not in and of itself an offence for a player to be in an offside position. It is only an offence if a player is offside and involved in active play. However, before 2005, 'involved in active play' was generally interpreted in a defence-friendly fashion, and in practice, attackers in an offside position were often penalised. The 2005 clarification changed that and set a higher bar for being involved in active play. In practice, it meant that players could drift offside without being penalised, as long as they didn't receive the ball, and in turn made it riskier for defences to employ an offside trap.

The football writer Jonathan Wilson has argued that this sequence of reforms has led to a well-balanced offside law that has changed the game for the better.[10] Back in 2005, football was dominated by tall, powerful attackers like Peter Crouch and Didier Drogba, and many fans and managers felt that smaller players were being muscled out of the game. With hindsight, this looks absurd: Lionel Messi was just about to explode onto the world stage, and Barcelona and Spain were on the verge of historic victories, won with a skilful passing game that did not depend on muscle.

Wilson's argument is that the 2005 changes to the offside law enabled these successes. By favouring the attacker, they made it harder for defences to employ the offside trap, and stretched the effective playing band of the pitch to about 70–80 metres, which in turn suited an intricate short passing game involving players who were good at finding and creating space.

Not everyone agrees with Wilson about the benign effects of these changes. Some argue that the 2005 offside law was overly complicated, difficult for fans to understand and referees to interpret. For others, this tinkering was the precursor to the greater confusion caused by VAR, and the first sign that something was going wrong with the laws of the game.

Still, whatever side of this debate you are on, it is probably fair to conclude that up until VAR was introduced, the offside law was interpreted in an attacker-friendly way that prevented goal-hanging, set the effective playing band at about 70–80 metres and made it risky to rely excessively on the offside trap.

Wilson's analysis of the law's changes over time also makes another important point: that the minutiae of many of the more recent, pro-attacking changes were too detailed to ever be implemented accurately by an on-field human referee in real time. In practice, what happened was that referees interpreted them to mean that they should give the benefit of any doubt to the attacker.

But now, of course, VAR has abolished doubt. We've applied the certainty and precision of technology to a law that was written in a pre-technology era. Heels, toes and armpits that would previously not have been noticed are now resulting in offside decisions.

The delicate 2005 balance has been upset, and the decades-long trend of favouring the attacker has been reversed. This is a major reason why Roy Hodgson and so many others feel that some of these tight offside calls are wrong. VAR is not enforcing the law in the way we were used to; instead, it is changing the way offside is interpreted to such an extent that it feels like the law itself has actually changed.

OFFSIDE IS NOT A COMPLETELY FACTUAL DECISION

Most offside controversies have been about close calls, factual decisions that felt too harsh. But further adding to the confusion, offside is not a completely factual decision.

It has subjective elements too. When referees decide whether a player is offside or not, they also have to make a judgement about whether the player is interfering with play. Being offside by itself is not an offence; it's only an offence if the player is interfering with play.

However, deciding what counts as interfering with play is subjective. Clearly, if a player touches the ball, they are interfering with play. If they are lying near the corner flag injured, they are not. But in between those two extremes are a number of different possible situations, some of which are quite hard to judge.

In Euro 2024, the Netherlands vs France match saw a lengthy VAR check over whether a player was interfering with play. Xavi Simons had scored for the Netherlands with a long-range shot. He was definitely not offside, but Denzil Dumfries, the Netherlands full-back, was. He was standing near France's goalkeeper, and the question was whether his position stopped the keeper from diving to save the ball. After nearly three minutes, the officials decided Dumfries was interfering with play, and so the goal should be disallowed.

The other subjective element is deciding when one phase of play ends and another starts. Because being offside is not an offence in itself, it is possible for a player to be offside and not interfering with play, then to come back into an onside position and score. Should they be penalised for the original offside? It depends on whether that particular phase of play has ended. Technically, a phase ends and a new one begins when a defending player touches the ball. This also means that if an attacker receives the ball directly from an opponent, he cannot be offside.

In June 2021, Kylian Mbappé scored for France against Spain in the Nations League. He ran on to a ball played through to him by his teammate Theo Hernández and was clearly offside as the pass was made. However, the pass took a slight deflection off the Spain defender Eric García, and that meant Mbappé was not offside. This was another case where, according to the letter of the law, the right decision was made, but where the letter of the law felt completely wrong. After a spate of similar decisions, IFAB updated the law to say that in a situation like this, a defending team would have to 'deliberately' play the ball in order for an attacker to be onside. A slight deflection like the one from García should result in an offside decision. But 'deliberately' is another word with a range of possible interpretations.

The two subjective aspects of the offside law have independently caused controversies of their own. But they also matter because they make it harder to devise general improvements to the offside decision-making system. For example, as we will see in Chapter 10, one possible solution is to automate offsides, making them more like goal-line decisions. But the subjective judgements about phases, opposition touches and interfering with play make automation much harder.

And the reason why automation matters, and why it is often proposed as a solution for offside, is because it would speed up decisions. That matters, because one of the most frequent criticisms of VAR has nothing to do with whether it results in the right decisions. It's that VAR's offside reviews take a long time to resolve and end up disrupting the flow of the game in a way that causes yet more problems. We'll consider this in the next chapter.

4

THE FLOW OF THE GAME

'Life can only be understood backwards, but it must be
lived forwards.'

Søren Kierkegaard

BREAKS IN PLAY

Sports like cricket, tennis and American football have a lot
of natural breaks, which make it easier to introduce video
review of decisions. Football is more fluid and unstructured,
which makes it harder to decide when a review should
take place and means that the reviews themselves often
interrupt the game. Before VAR, most of the video review
debate was about whether it would lead to more correct
decisions. After VAR, we realised that getting more correct
decisions can't be the sole criterion by which we measure
its success. Other things matter too. The interruptions to

the game and the time it takes for VAR to do its work have caused many more problems than anyone anticipated.

PROBLEM ONE: THE TIME IT TAKES TO MAKE A DECISION

The most straightforward VAR incidents are those where the ball goes out of play straight after the incident, where it's obvious to everyone that something needs to be reviewed and the review therefore happens straight away. But even these decisions can take a long time. The longest VAR review in the Premier League came in 2023–24, for an offside check that ruled out a Jay Rodriguez goal for Burnley. It took a total of five minutes – over 5% of a football match. The average time for a VAR review in 2023–24 was 64 seconds, up from 40 seconds the season before. This increase is yet more evidence that VAR is not overcoming its teething problems, but rather discovering new difficulties as it goes along.

PROBLEM TWO: THE TIME IT TAKES BEFORE EVERYONE REALISES THAT THERE IS A DECISION TO BE MADE

Sometimes fans celebrate for a long time before realising that a VAR check is happening. In 2018–19, in the first year of VAR's operation in the Champions League, Manchester

City thought they had won a pulsating quarter-final against Spurs with a last-minute goal from Raheem Sterling. Their fans celebrated wildly, the Spurs players slumped to the floor, and a solid minute passed before anyone even realised the goal was being checked. The review found that Sergio Agüero was offside in the build-up, so the goal was disallowed. In the time between the ball hitting the back of the net and the goal being overturned, one City fan had left the ground, hoping to beat the crowds, and had to be told by a cameraman that his team had not won the match. His crestfallen reaction went viral on social media.

But things have not improved since then. In 2023–24, Coventry City fans celebrated wildly and enthusiastically after they thought they had scored a famous last-minute winner against Manchester United in the FA Cup semi-final. Again, significant time elapsed between the ball hitting the back of the net and fans realising it was being checked. The goal was disallowed, and Coventry eventually lost the match.

Perhaps fans and players will stop celebrating in real time. In May 2021, the West Ham striker Michail Antonio scored twice against Burnley but barely celebrated either goal, despite the fact that he is known for his zany celebrations. After the match, when an interviewer asked him why, he said that he had stopped celebrating goals because of the risk of looking stupid when they are ruled out by VAR.

PROBLEM THREE: 'GHOST MINUTES' THAT DISAPPEAR AFTER A VAR REVIEW

If the ball goes out of play straight after a VAR incident, it's easy to keep play paused while the review takes place. But sometimes the ball does not go out, and the game carries on while the incident is being reviewed. If it turns out there was an infringement, then everything in between the incident and the ball eventually going out of play gets cancelled.

The most famous example of this came in a February 2020 Premier League match between Manchester City and Spurs. Sergio Agüero was fouled in the box, but no penalty was given by the on-field referee, and the game continued for two minutes before the ball went out of play. In that time, the VAR had reviewed the foul and decided it was a penalty. The two minutes of play that happened after the foul were deleted from the records. They are referred to in the law as the 'post-incident period'. If Spurs had scored a goal in that time, it would not have counted. However, certain disciplinary actions *would* still have counted: for example, if a player had been sent off for violent conduct in those two minutes, the red card would have stood.

PROBLEM FOUR: THE 'GHOST MINUTES' PROBLEM IS EXACERBATED BY THE 'LATE FLAG'

In 2020–21, the second year of VAR's operation in the Premier League, the guidelines about offside were adjusted, and the on-field assistant referee was instructed to delay such decisions. This is because the VAR cannot review something that happens *after* the on-field officials have stopped play. It's a crucial change that has important analogues in other sports, so it's worth exploring further.

Here's a simple example of what this law change was trying to prevent:

Team A are the defending side. Team B are on the attack. Team B's striker runs on to a through ball and slots it beyond the goalkeeper into the net.

However, as striker B ran on to the ball, and before he touched it, the assistant referee flagged for offside, and the referee blew his whistle to stop play.* Team A therefore stopped playing, and their goalkeeper did not attempt to save the shot.

But a replay shows that striker B was not, in fact, offside.

What should happen now? There are two options, but only one is possible, given football's laws.

---

* The assistant referee's flag does not on its own stop play. The referee's whistle does. But in most cases the referee will blow his whistle after seeing the flag.

- Goal awarded to Team B. This cannot happen, according to the laws, because the whistle blew before the goal was scored, and Team A stopped playing when they heard it. The keeper didn't dive, and the defenders didn't try to tackle. However, even if the keeper hadn't heard the whistle and did keep playing, it doesn't matter. The whistle did blow, so it can't be a goal.
- No goal awarded. This is the only legitimate option, given football's laws, but it feels unfair on Team B. They had a fantastic, legitimate chance to score, which was taken away from them due to a refereeing error, and which cannot now be given back to them.

This is a horrible situation. You cannot possibly award the goal, because play was stopped by the on-field officials before the goal was scored. VAR can go back in time to review a decision, but it cannot change what happened as a consequence of that decision.

There are interesting analogues in other sports. Here is a similar one in cricket: Team A is the batting side. Team B is fielding. Team A needs four runs off the last ball to win. Bowler B bowls a good in-swinging yorker. Batter A jams down his bat, and the ball squirts away into the outfield, in between the slips. The umpire determines that the ball has hit the pad first and gives the batter out, leg before wicket. Team B celebrate and do not bother fielding the ball, which has run away in between the fielders to the boundary rope.

Batter A thinks that he hit the ball with his bat first. He appeals the umpire's decision, and it turns out he is right. He is not out.

What should happen now? There are two possible options, but again, only one is possible given cricket's laws.

- Batter A is not out and is awarded four runs. This cannot happen, according to the laws, because as soon as the umpire made the on-field out decision, the ball was deemed to be dead. Team B stopped trying to field the ball when they saw the out decision. Had they known the batter was not out, they would have kept playing and might have prevented the boundary. But even if they had continued, it wouldn't have mattered. The umpire gave it out, which meant the ball was dead.
- Batter A is not out and is awarded no runs. This is the only legitimate option, given cricket's laws, but it feels unfair on Team A. If the umpire had given the correct on-field decision, he would have got four runs, and his team would have won the match. Instead, they have lost.

There are similar situations in tennis, but tennis has different ways of responding:

Two tennis players are exchanging groundstrokes. Player B is well on top in the rally. He is moving player

A all over the court, and it seems only a matter of time before player A loses the point. Player B plays a great shot down the line, which player A has little chance of reaching. However, the shot is called out by the line judge, so player A wins the point. Player B reviews the line call, and it turns out it was in.

What should happen now?

There are two options, analogous to the football and cricket ones:

- Player B could win the point. They hit a great shot, but player A stopped playing when they heard the line judge call it out. They might have been able to return the ball if they'd kept playing.
- Player A could win the point. This feels totally wrong. Player B's shot was in, so how can it be fair for player A to win the point?

But in tennis, there are two other options, options that are not available to cricket and football officials. The tennis chair umpire *does* have the power to imagine the future and award the point to player B, if they feel there was really no chance that player A could have returned the ball.

And, if the chair umpire is not sure whether player A would have made the return, they can decide to replay the point.

The other crucial difference with tennis is that these exact same dilemmas existed before the player review system was introduced, because in the pre-review world the chair umpire could overrule the line judge. In this sense, decision review in tennis has not caused the same fraying of the historic laws as it has in football and cricket, because a non-technological decision review process already existed, and the laws of the game were already designed to deal with it.

With football and cricket, decision review has solved – or at least tried to – the issue of incorrect decisions. But in doing so, it has created completely new problems that are hard to fix without changing some fundamental aspects of the laws.

It is relatively straightforward to change a decision, but it is impossible to change the impact that decision had on the behaviour of the players. Football Team A's goalkeeper stopped playing when he saw the offside flag. Cricket Team B stopped fielding when they saw the umpire give the batter out.

Video reviews can do many things, but they cannot turn back time.

In cricket, perhaps you could borrow tennis's solution and allow the ball to be re-bowled, or even let the umpire make a judgement call about what would have happened if the decision had gone the other way.

In football, that's not possible. You can't 'replay the point', and letting the referee make a judgement call about what might have happened would be wildly controversial.

But there is one simple tweak that feels like it can fix the problem – which is for the on-field official to delay their decision. Those decisions can then be reviewed *after* the phase of play has ended. If a player truly is offside, the defending team would get a free kick. If they were actually onside, the attacking team wouldn't have been denied the benefit of a possible goal-scoring opportunity.

In theory, this feels like quite a sensible move. In practice, it has caused far more problems than anyone anticipated. True, it works well for the scenario where a striker bursts through on goal and shoots in one rapid phase of play. But there are many more possible situations, including some where play goes on for quite a long time after the original offside decision was made, thus creating more ghost-minute problems.

Not only that, but when obvious offsides are not flagged, you often get chaos, as the attacking player will typically be metres ahead of the defence, defenders will have to sprint back to make desperate last-ditch tackles and goalkeepers will have to run out to challenge the attacker. And this will all happen with both sets of players not being quite sure what is going on. You can sometimes see players looking round, thinking, *Is this real? Is it actually worth me trying to cross the ball or beat the man here? Do I need to put in a tackle, or can I just let it go?*

Again, within a few months of the new law coming into effect, problems were piling up. In one match between

Manchester United and Liverpool in January 2021, in the first half alone there were three late flags that led to chaotic periods of play. Teams like Liverpool, who play a high defensive line and have full-backs who switch rapidly from defence to attack, and vice versa, were particularly stung by the law change.

After that match, the Liverpool full-back Andy Robertson said, 'Sometimes the momentum of the game can change because they get belief that they've just had a shot on goal and we think he's three yards offside so why hasn't it stopped. [For] one of them, Trent sprinted back 40 yards to try and slide tackle and he's miles offside, so Trent's done an extra sprint and was then out of position – so it is frustrating.'

The simple tweak of the delayed flag has exacerbated the ghost-minutes problem, creating lots more moments that might or might not be real. Not only that, but while this tweak was designed to *reduce* the stakes of the original decision, it has actually ended up *increasing* them. There have been a number of marginal offside calls that, if they had been made straightaway, would have been entirely uncontroversial because they wouldn't have seemed that significant. They would have interrupted the attacking stage fairly early on.

But once you know that a simple pass early in an attack has led to a goal, suddenly the stakes are much higher. This was part of the problem with the disallowed Coventry goal against Manchester United in the 2024 FA Cup semi-final. Procedurally, it was an example of the late flag working well. It was a marginal decision, so the on-field official delayed it until after the phase of play was complete. But if he had flagged at the moment of the infringement, we'd never have known whether that phase would have led to a goal, so the decision wouldn't have been nearly as controversial. The late flag extended an alternative timeline of joy to Coventry fans, only to snatch it away.

Delaying a decision is not a neutral act; it's a decision in itself, one that opens up alternative timelines.

PROBLEM FIVE: ASSISTANT REFEREES ARE NOT CAPABLE OF FLAGGING LATE RELIABLY

After the first year of the new late-flag directive, the chaos and ghost minutes brought about another tweak to the laws. The PGMOL raised the threshold for when an official should delay flagging. They should do so only if it looked like there was an immediate and obvious goal-scoring opportunity. On all other occasions, they didn't need to delay.

But real-time offside decisions already involve a lot of cognitive capacity. To what extent are assistant referees going to be able to reliably identify immediate and obvious goal-scoring opportunities, given everything else they have to think about with offside?

Entirely predictably, we soon had an example of an assistant referee immediately flagging a marginal offside moments before a goal was scored. And on review, the player turned out to be onside. In September 2022, Philippe Coutinho scored a superb goal for Aston Villa against Manchester City – except it didn't count, as the flag went up and the whistle blew just before his shot. On review, it turned out he was actually onside.

Unless you have a blanket ban on on-field flags, you will always run the risk of the assistant referee making an error, flagging when they shouldn't, and there being nothing that VAR can do about it.

But if you have a blanket ban, then there would be the risk of lots of ghost minutes, causing plenty of confusion.

As ever with VAR, we seem to have the worst of both worlds, as can be seen from some high-profile incidents from the 2023–24 season. In the Premier League, assistant referees seem to be cautious about raising their flags, and this led to two chaotic incidents, where two Manchester City players sustained bad injuries. In December 2023, the City keeper Ederson injured himself after sprinting from his goal line and colliding with Kyle Walker and Sean Longstaff in an effort to prevent Newcastle scoring from a counter-attack. But it turned out that Longstaff and Alexander Isak were both offside at the start of the move. In January 2024, John Stones injured himself after sprinting back and putting in a last-ditch tackle on the Everton striker Beto, who, it turned out, was in an offside position.

In the second leg of the Champions League semi-final between Real Madrid and Bayern Munich in May 2024, we saw how delaying flags can work – and also how it doesn't.

In the 91st minute, Joselu scored for Real Madrid. The assistant referee thought it was offside, but he delayed the flag until after the goal was scored to allow VAR to check it. VAR said it was onside. This was a textbook example of how it can be good to delay the flag.

In the 101st minute, Matthijs de Ligt scored for Bayern Munich. The assistant referee thought that Noussair Mazraoui was offside in the build-up but did *not* delay his flag. He flagged the instant the offence was committed, and the referee blew his whistle. The decision, therefore, could not be reviewed by VAR, but TV replays showed it was incredibly tight and may well have been onside. The Bayern Munich manager Thomas Tuchel called the decision 'disastrous' and 'against every rule'.

This was the sixth full season VAR had been operational in the Champions League. If anything, it now felt more confusing, complicated and chaotic than when it was first introduced.

SPORT IS SYNCHRONOUS, AND REVIEWS ARE ASYNCHRONOUS

The cricket writer Kartikeya Date has written perceptively about this problem in cricket. He notes that cricket's dead-ball law is fundamental to the game. Likewise, in football, the on-field whistle to stop play is crucial too. It is hard to imagine how the game would work without there being an on-field official who has a mechanism to stop and start the game. Generations of players have grown up being told that you play to the whistle, with the implication being that once it sounds, the game stops. A decision review system can decide the referee was wrong to blow the whistle, but it cannot change the way the players behaved after the whistle was blown.

Sport is real-time and synchronous. Reviews are retrospective and asynchronous. Decision review systems are attempting to graft retrospective technological reviews on top of pre-existing laws that were designed to work in real time.

What's the way out of this problem? You can't change sport so that it doesn't happen in real time. But can you change the technology so that it works in real time? That's what tennis is doing. Many tournaments now use computer vision technology to make all the line calls in real time, instead of using it to retrospectively to challenge human decisions. Football already has a bit of this too: one reason goal-line technology works so well is that it is more or less instantaneous. But would this ever be possible for other decisions, like offside, handball and foul play? We'll consider that in Part 2.

One low-tech solution is to ask the referees to hurry up. But that has its own problems, as we will see in the next chapter.

5

HUMAN ERROR

'For the simplicity on this side of complexity, I wouldn't give you
a fig. But for the simplicity on the other side of complexity, for
that I would give you anything I have.'

Oliver Wendell Holmes

TO ERR IS HUMAN

Humans make errors. This is a well-known fact, and we
have a number of stock phrases that express this point:
'I'm only human'; 'Nobody's perfect'; 'Everybody makes
mistakes'; 'To err is human, to forgive, divine'.

The argument in favour of technology in sport is that
because humans make errors, they need help.

But VAR hasn't eliminated human error. In fact, it's created brand-new mistakes, of a type we haven't seen before.

In 2023, there were three glaring human errors in the use of the VAR system itself:

- In the Arsenal vs Brentford match on 11 February, the video assistant referee ran an offside check on Ethan Pinnock after a Brentford goal. He forgot to run one on Pinnock's teammate Christian Nørgaard later in the same phase. Nørgaard was offside, so if the check had been made, the goal would have been disallowed.
- At the Crystal Palace vs Brighton match on the same day, the video assistant referee checked if Brighton's Pervis Estupiñán was offside. He drew the offside line from the Palace defender James Tomkins. But Tomkins's teammate Marc Guéhi was standing behind Tomkins and playing Estupiñán on. The goal was ruled out for offside, but it should have been awarded.
- On 30 September, a match between Spurs and Liverpool saw perhaps the biggest VAR error ever. Luis Díaz scored but was immediately flagged offside by the on-field assistant referee. Darren England, the video assistant referee, checked the decision and realised Díaz was onside. However, he did not realise that the original on-field decision was offside, thinking a goal had been awarded. So he told the on-field team, 'Check complete,' meaning their original decision was correct. They restarted play and did not award a goal. A few

seconds after the restart, England realised what had happened – but it was too late to do anything about it at that point.

All three errors caused storms of outrage and demands for the games to be replayed. All three also took place in 2023, four years after the introduction of VAR, when all the teething problems were supposed to have been resolved.

At the start of this book, we looked at one of the most famous pre-VAR errors, Thierry Henry's handball against Ireland. In this case, there was little that the referee could have done differently. He was positioned in a sensible place, given what was happening on the pitch, but there were some players in between him and Henry, and he simply could not see what had occurred. You can perhaps argue that he should have positioned himself differently or moved quicker, but in a fluid, fast-moving sport like football there will always be times when the on-field referee cannot get a perfect view of what has happened, and there will always be times when this leads to mistakes. Similarly, there will always be errors when making on-field offside decisions, because offside is often beyond the limits of human judgement.

We can call mistakes like this errors of incapacity. Human beings simply do not have the capacity to see through solid objects, to fly, to run 60 metres in one second or to look at two things at once. If you want to fix such errors, you have to enhance human capacity with the use of technology, like video replays.

However, there is another type of human error: errors of ineptitude or incompetence, where although humans have the capacity and skill to do something correctly, they still get it wrong.

The three errors at the start of this chapter fall into this category. It is *possible* for officials to communicate clearly. It is *possible* for video assistant referees to identify the correct players when making an offside decision. The reasons for these failures are not down to fundamental limitations in our capacity.

When you talk to people about the Thierry Henry handball and show them the video of it, they'll often say, 'Well, you can't really blame the ref there.' If he physically could not see the handball, what could he do? You can't blame someone for something that is impossible.

But when you talk to people about the Nørgaard, Estupiñán and Díaz errors, that's not the reaction they have. They blame the officials, because the errors were avoidable. There are plenty of examples of referees being faced with similar decisions and making them correctly.

Something similar holds with medical errors. If a patient dies of a disease that has no known cure, we don't blame the doctor. If a patient dies of a disease that can be cured but the doctor fails to do so because they misdiagnose the illness, haven't heard of the cure or mess up its

administration, then we do blame them, and quite frequently we sue them too.

The incapacity/incompetence division is a useful one.
But if we think about it more deeply, are errors of incom-
petence actually more avoidable than errors of incapacity?
We might expect the majority of the Nørgaard/Estupiñán/
Diaz-type decisions to be made correctly, but is it realistic
to expect 100% or even 99% accuracy?

I would argue that it isn't. Humans do make mistakes,
and we aren't 100% competent. If you build a system that
depends on humans never making errors of incompetence,
your system will not work reliably. Expecting 99%-plus
levels of competence is actually as unrealistic as expecting
a human to have X-ray vision. It is as fundamentally inhu-
man to never make errors of incompetence as it is to be
able to look in two places at once.

If humans are so error-prone, how is it possible for
highly reliable systems to exist? After all, many systems do
achieve 99%-plus levels of accuracy, despite having many
vital roles played by humans. The most obvious example
is aviation. In 2023, there were 37.7 million plane journeys,
and just one fatal accident. Lots of the work involved in
building and flying planes is automated, but humans still
do crucial, complex jobs. Given what I have said about
human incompetence, how is this possible? If we can land
nearly 40 million planes safely, surely we can draw the lines
for few hundred offside decisions correctly?

THE POWER OF THE CHECKLIST

Many people are interested in the secrets of aviation's success. The surgeon Atul Gawande has written an entire book about what medicine could learn from aviation, and it's called *The Checklist Manifesto*, because Gawande's argument is that the humble checklist is one of the major factors in aviation's incredible safety record. Its power lies in its ability to reduce or eliminate errors of incompetence, the small things that you know you should have done but, for whatever reason, didn't.

Gawande points out that airplane take-off checklists consist of what might be thought of as 'dumb stuff': reminders to 'check that the brakes are released, that the instruments are set, that the door and windows are closed, that the elevator controls are unlocked'. But these checklists make a huge difference to safety, because in complex environments it is easy to overlook a simple step. Likewise, in medicine, a simple five-step checklist dramatically reduces the rate of catheter infections. Gawande also explains that checklists are particularly valuable when skipping just one step will doom your entire enterprise:Faulty memory and distraction are a particular danger in what engineers call all-or-none processes: whether running to the store to buy ingredients for a cake, preparing an airplane for takeoff, or evaluating a sick person in the hospital, if you miss just one key thing, you might as well not have made the effort at all.

That's exactly what happened with the three errors of incompetence listed at the start of this chapter. In each case, the video assistant referee does everything right, apart from one thing, but that one thing sinks everything.

VAR does have its own version of a checklist: 'protocols'. Other sports have something similar. In cricket and rugby, when you listen in to the conversations between officials, you can tell they are following a checklist. Each decision follows a similar sequence, and there are set phrases that have a specific meaning. For example, in cricket, the TV umpire will state what the review's about and the original decision and then check for a fair delivery. In rugby, when checking a try, the on-field official has specific pre-set questions they can ask the Television Match Official.

In football, the officials' discussions are not relayed live to either fans in the ground or those at home. For the first three seasons of VAR, recordings were not released afterwards either. However, in 2023–24, after a spate of errors, the PGMOL decided to release the recordings from selected incidents and have the body's head, Howard Webb, discuss them on TV.

One of the recordings selected for release was the Luis Díaz offside against Spurs. The two-minute clip reveals that the video assistant referee, Darren England, correctly identifies quite quickly that Diaz is onside and that his goal should stand. But he either doesn't realise or forgets that the original decision by the on-field team was offside. So instead of asking the on-field team to overturn their original decision, he tells them to keep it.

Compared with audio from rugby and cricket, there are a few differences. First, while rugby and cricket discussions are heavily structured and routinised, the football discussion felt like an unstructured chat. Perhaps there is a communication protocol, but it was hard to spot. At the start of every cricket review, the TV umpire restates the original decision, saying something along the lines of, 'We have a player review for lbw, the original decision is not out.' If football had a simple routine like this, it might have prevented the Díaz error from happening.

Second, there are many people involved in the football discussion. On the Díaz recording, there are a total of four different people speaking: the on-field referee, the video assistant referee, the assistant video assistant referee and the replay operator. This inevitably increases the potential for confusion.

Third, the on-field referee can't hear everything the off-field team say. This is a deliberate design decision that allows the on-field referee to focus on the match while checks are carrying on in the background. But again, it obviously increases the potential for errors and reduces the understanding between the two teams.

Fourth, the off-field officials are obviously rushing. They want to allow play to restart as quickly as possible, which is completely understandable, given all the problems with lengthy checks bogging down the flow of the game. But when you speed up a process, it can make human error more likely.

From the outside, the whole set-up feels like a recipe for error and confusion. After listening to it, I felt that the surprising thing was not that there have been so many VAR errors, but that there have been so few.

So, who is to blame?

After the Díaz incident, the processes behind VAR came under a lot of scrutiny. When discussing the error, Howard Webb said that VAR *did* have protocols for decision-making, and the problem was that they were not followed by the video assistant referee.

This is a bit of a circular argument. The point of a protocol is to prevent human error. If it is easily defeated by human error, it is legitimate to ask if the protocol is as good as it could be.

Again, aviation does not seem to have this problem. There are multiple checklists, and you rarely hear stories about pilots or air traffic controllers not following them properly. How does aviation make the protocols that guard against error work?

Back to Gawande. Fired up by his research about the power of checklists, he went back to his hospital and designed one for surgery. It was nothing like as successful as he had hoped. It wasn't clear who was supposed to go through the checklist, many of the checks were ambiguous, it took too long to use, and it distracted the clinicians from the patient on the operating table, who sensed the uncertainty and confusion. Gawande's team abandoned the checklist before the end of its first day. It's really easy to write a checklist, but really hard to write a good one. And when you write a bad checklist, what happens? People ignore it.

The PGMOL refer to their VAR protocols a lot, but they don't publish them, so it's hard to know exactly what they include and what format they take. But it's plausible to speculate that the protocols are a bit vague, a bit time-consuming, a bit unclear, and so in the heat of the moment they get skipped. I think many people in sectors outside aviation may have had a similar experience at work. Some kind of process is dreamt up by a senior team in an office, the professionals at the workplace roll their eyes and use it a few times to make the bosses happy, but as soon as the pressure is on it gets forgotten. In fact, it is this kind of bureaucratic paperwork that often makes front-line professionals loathe their desk-bound colleagues.

But in aviation, front-line professionals don't ignore the checklists. Black box recordings of flight emergencies show that even in the most extreme circumstances, flight crew follow checklists, often with a remarkable degree of success. Why is aviation different? Gawande asks exactly that question, and the answer takes him on a tour of what he calls 'checklist factories' – the institutions that are responsible for creating them. He discovers that creating a good checklist is not easy. Although most of them consist of just six to nine items, they need enormous amounts of planning, analysis and iteration:

> You must define a clear pause point at which the checklist is supposed to be used (unless the moment is obvious, like when a warning light goes on or an engine fails). You must decide whether you want a DO-CONFIRM checklist or a READ-DO checklist. With a DO-CONFIRM checklist [. . .] team members perform their jobs from memory and experience, often separately. But then they stop. They pause to run the checklist and confirm that everything that was supposed to be done was done. With a READ-DO checklist, on the other hand, people carry out the tasks as they check them off – it's more like a recipe. So for any new checklist created from scratch, you have to pick the type that makes the most sense for the situation.

They also need to be tested in the real world:

> No matter how careful we might be, no matter how much thought we might put in, a checklist has to be tested in the real world, which is inevitably more complicated than expected. First drafts always fall apart [. . .]

and one needs to study how, make changes, and keep testing until the checklist works consistently.

Interestingly, the team of cricket officials who helped develop the Decision Review System also seem to have been influenced by aviation checklists. Simon Taufel, a former Test umpire, compared the development of DRS protocols to air traffic control:

> Businesses that need to focus on communicating effectively, something like air traffic control, use agreed terminology and work with non-English speaking people.

He also said that whilst the DRS scripts can sound quite robotic and stereotyped, that's a deliberate strategy to reduce error:

> It can come across as robotic, but when you have very clear, agreed communication phrases of introduction, identification, requests and acknowledgement, then you leave very little room for human error and misunderstanding.[11]

SYSTEMS VS PEOPLE

Checklists are part of a broader and more systemic approach to preventing error that focuses on systems

rather than people. One leading expert in the field, James
Reason, has written a paper explaining how a system
approach to error prevention works, contrasting it with
what he calls a 'person approach'.[12] The more traditional
person approach focuses on the people at the sharp end:
front-line professionals like doctors, nurses, pilots – and,
one might add, referees. By contrast, the system approach
accepts that human error will always be with us and
focuses instead on creating systems that prevent those
errors from creating catastrophes. 'Though we cannot
change the human condition,' says Reason, 'we can change
the conditions under which humans work.' Checklists are
an important part of those systems.

The system approach has a tremendous amount of evidence on its side, but it can be controversial. There are two
common critiques. One is that it denies individual accountability. A person can make really bad, egregious errors
and then just turn around and blame 'the system'. At its
worst, the system approach can sound like the Nuremberg
defence: 'I was only following orders. It's the system's fault,
not my own. I didn't really have a choice.'

You can also argue that if you reduce accountability,
you make individual errors more likely. If people know
that they are not going to be held accountable for errors,
they are more likely to become lazy and sloppy. The social
psychologist Jonathan Haidt has argued that the way to
create an ethical society is 'to make sure that everyone's

reputation is on the line all the time, so that bad behaviour will always bring bad consequences'.[13] We'll consider this idea more closely in Chapter 11.

However, the system approach to error prevention is not opposed to individual accountability; it is just more likely to focus on the senior managers who are responsible for badly designed processes than on the front-line professionals who deal with the consequences of these processes. Reason's contrast between the person approach and the system approach is perhaps misleading. A better way of thinking about it might be front-line professional versus senior manager.

Similarly, the system approach does not deny the use of penalties for certain types of individual misbehaviour. If a particular system depends on people showing up for work sober, then it can be appropriate to have sanctions for those who turn up drunk. It's just that the system approach would say that it would also be sensible to have other safeguards in place, so that if a drunk person does turn up for work, they do not end up operating dangerous machinery.

The second critique of the system approach comes from front-line professionals themselves. Even though they are the most likely to suffer unfairly under a person-based approach, they can often be the most resistant to a system approach. It is not hard to see why. Think back to Gawande's explanation of what happens when you use a bad checklist, and the challenges involved in creating a good one.

Creating a good checklist requires asking front-line professionals to repeat their most basic routines over and over again in an attempt to codify them, tweak those routines based on feedback from other people, and then practise the new ones religiously so they become second nature. None of this is fun. Nobody likes it. It's exhausting to have to rethink your most basic habits. Everyone will come up with reasons why other people have to do it, and why they are a special case who deserves exemption.

Institutional pressures also make it hard to establish new systems. Sometimes there are hierarchical tensions between different professionals. Nurses and junior doctors can be reluctant to correct a more senior medic, while consultants from one specialism might be less likely to accept the findings from another. One of aviation's successes has been in breaking down hierarchies and empowering junior members of staff to speak up to senior pilots.

At other times, professional autonomy can get in the way of the consistency and collaboration required to make a system work. This is common in education, where there is a romantic idea of the autonomous, creative teacher inspiring their class with hand-crafted lesson plans.

More prosaically, people think checklists are for dummies. They sound so infantilising. Maybe they are good for trainees, but there's a feeling that a true professional shouldn't need one; that you don't need to tick off that step because it's blindingly obvious. Spending large amounts of time creating a foolproof system suggests that you think your colleagues are fools.

But the insights from all the research is that if making errors makes you a fool, then we are all fools. Pilots, doctors, referees . . . all human beings, however skilled and expert, are capable of making simple errors that have big consequences. If we want to stop the mistakes, then first of all we have to acknowledge that.

For me, the biggest piece of evidence in favour of the system approach and against the person approach is that the former works so well in aviation, which is a sector that has the most extreme levels of personal accountability. In aviation, if you make a mistake, you die. Flight crew are not just responsible for other people's lives, but their own too. And yet aviation is the sector that has most embraced the system approach, and in doing so has perhaps had more success than any other sector in reducing error and creating scalable and consistent processes. When it is your own life on the line, you want a checklist.

Checklists are an important method for reducing human error. But given the tendency of humans to make errors, another way of reducing them is just to reduce the role played by humans. If you can replace a human with an algorithm or an automated process, you take away a lot of the potential for errors and inconsistency. We'll look at the advantages and disadvantages of automation in Chapter 9.

VAR has complicated decisions concerning handball, foul play and offside, it's disrupted the flow of the game, and it's multiplied the opportunities for human error. In Part 2, I will look at ways of solving these problems.

PART 2
SOLUTIONS

6

CONTINUUMS AND CATEGORIES

'But to understand God's thoughts, we must study statistics, for these are the measure of His purpose.'

Florence Nightingale

DIFFERENT TYPES OF CATEGORY

Imagine you are filling in an online form. It asks the following questions: How long have you been doing your current job? What date did you move into your current home? How far is your home from the nearest train station?

The answers to these questions are continuous variables. You might have worked at your current job for six years and 234 days. You might have moved into your house seven years and 20 days ago. Your home might be 875 metres from the nearest train station. Continuous variables can represent any value along a continuum, and they can be divided into fractions. We deal with them every day, most frequently when we have to measure time and distance.

The form goes on to ask more questions. Do you own a mobile phone? Do you live in the UK? Do you normally wear glasses or contact lenses? The answers to these questions are categorical variables. You can put people into two or three categories based on their answers to these questions. You can count categorical variables, but you measure continuous variables.

There is one final question on the form: Are you aged over 18? This is also a categorical variable, but it's not quite like the other categories. In this case, the category has been superimposed on top of a continuous variable. Age is a continuous variable, but the person asking this question isn't interested in your precise age. They just want to know if you are over 18 or not. They've split the continuous variable of age into two categories.

A lot of the decisions football referees have to make are like this. They involve putting an incident into two categories, but those categories are drawn on top of a smooth continuum. Goals are the obvious example: we literally draw a line on the pitch to determine where the ball has to go for it to be a goal. We've chopped up the continuous distribution of space into different categories.

In football, and in life, such divisions are necessary and unavoidable. If you don't have a goal line, you don't have a game. Similarly, most countries use age cut-offs for a variety of different purposes. In England, the age cut-off for buying alcohol is 18, and schools place all the students born between 1 September and 31 August into the same school year. But scientists and statisticians don't like it when you divide up continuums like this. The division introduces distortions and means you throw away potentially useful information. You don't magically turn into a different person the day you turn 18. Some 17.5-year-olds are more mature and sensible than many 18.5-year-olds. A child born on 31 August 2017 is closer in age to one born on 1 September 2017 than to most of the children in their actual school year.

THE TYRANNY OF THE DISCONTINUOUS MIND

In an article from 2011, the biologist Richard Dawkins wrote about what he calls 'the tyranny of the discontinuous mind'.[14] This is when we forget that many categories are just arbitrary lines on top of a continuum. Dawkins gives some startling examples: we think of different species of animals as being categorically different from each other, but they are not really.

It's easy for us to assume fish and humans are categorically different because the forms of life in between the two no longer exist. But in fact, fish and humans are just at different points on a continuum of life forms.

This is theoretically interesting but unlikely to cause many problems in day-to-day life. But Dawkins also gives some examples of the tyranny of the discontinuous mind causing real problems. Often, scientists are asked to decide if new drugs or technologies are safe or not. But safety and risk are continuous variables, not categorical ones. Dawkins also mentions educational assessment as another field that relies too heavily on continuum cut-offs. Many assessment systems put students into grade categories, and then assume that all those with an A are qualitatively different to those with a B. But student attainment is on a smooth continuum. The difference between a student with the bottom A-grade and one with the top B-grade is one mark, not some ineffable difference in their quality of thought.

THE CHAOS OF THE CONTINUOUS MIND

Still, while I think Dawkins is right to complain about the tyranny of the discontinuous mind, we should also acknowledge the opposite cognitive distortion, one we might call 'the chaos of the continuous mind'. This is when you get so carried away with the fact that continuous distributions are continuous that you forget that there are still extremes. Humans and fish are still different animals that cannot interbreed, even if there is an unbroken line of descent between them. Blue and red still exist, even if there are many shades of purple in between. And there will always be times in our imperfect world when we have to draw a line on continuous distribution, because the alternative would be complete chaos.

Age limits are the most common practical example of categories being imposed on a continuous distribution, and most people tend to accept them without falling for either cognitive distortion. We know that there is no qualitative difference in physical and intellectual capacity between the average person aged 17 years and 364 days and the average person aged 18 years and zero days. But we also realise that we have to place a cut-off for buying alcohol *somewhere*, otherwise we will let five-year-olds buy whisky.

LINE CALLS

Most people have a similarly sensible attitude when it comes to goal-line decisions. We don't fall into the tyranny of the discontinuous mind by pretending to ourselves that there is something rarefied about the air or the grass on one side of a line, but not on the other. But nor do we fall into the chaos of the continuous mind by saying that if a ball gets close to the line, it should count as a goal because it's only a few millimetres away. We understand that while the line is fairly arbitrary, it is necessary for the game to work.

However, there are other judgements where we do stray into error. We are much more likely to fall into the chaos of the continuous mind when thinking about offside. As we saw in Chapter 3, players, fans and managers can all be found bemoaning the way that goals are being ruled in and out based on toenails, armpits and other similarly tiny margins, when if they made the same argument about goal-line decisions they would get laughed at.

MISTAKEN IDENTITIES

What about the other kinds of decisions referees have to make? One example of a true categorical decision is that of identity. In 2014, the Arsenal player Kieran Gibbs was sent off for a handball in the penalty area, when it was actually Alex Oxlade-Chamberlain who handled the ball. That's a true categorical decision – and in this case, a categorical error. Alex Oxlade-Chamberlain is Alex Oxlade-Chamberlain. He's not 'nearly' Kieran Gibbs. There are no close calls with mistaken identities. You can't say, 'Well, it was only *just* a case of mistaken identity,' in the way that you can say, 'It was *just* one centimetre over the line,' or '*just* one centimetre offside'.

WHAT ABOUT FOULS?

So, offsides and goal-line decisions are categories imposed on continuums. Identity decisions are true categories.

What about fouls? Are they more like goal-line decisions, or are they more like identities?

I think they are categories imposed on a continuum. Some incidents, like Thierry Henry's handball, are at one extreme of being obvious foul play. Others, where the ball has not touched a player's arm at all, are at the other extreme of definitely not being a foul. In between are a whole series of incidents that are not as much of a foul as Henry's handball, but still more of a foul than nothing at all.

I think it is difficult for us to accept that fouls are a continuum because, unlike with goal-line decisions and offside, we have no underlying metric that we can use to measure the continuum. We can't measure fouls by the millimetre, the way we measure offsides and balls over the goal-line. The only device we have to help the referee measure is the rule book. And as we will see in the next chapter, rule books make poor metrics.

When we don't have a good measurement for a continuum and the only thing we care about is sorting things into two categories, then it can be tempting to forget about the continuum and just come up with a way of sorting things into two categories. But this is a mistake. Even if we need only a categorical judgement, we should acknowledge that the underlying scale is continuous, because that will help us make the categorical judgement.

Here is an analogy: imagine you work in a supermarket

and have to check the ages of people buying alcohol. Suppose every person who tries to buy alcohol has a passport with their exact date of birth on it, which they are happy to show you. Your decisions will be quite straightforward. The footballing equivalent is goal-line decisions. In both cases, you have to make a judgement about a cut-off line on a continuum, and in both, you have very reliable measurements and instruments to help you.

Now suppose that every person who tries to buy alcohol has a passport that they are happy to show you, but it features only their year of birth, not the exact date. Having the passport is better than nothing, and it will help you resolve most decisions, but there will be some tricky ones where you still won't be sure whether the person is over 18 or not. The footballing equivalent is offside decisions using VAR technology. The technology is better than human judgement, but it still leaves room for doubt and argument.

Now suppose that every person who tries to buy alcohol has no passport, and you have to make the judgement just by looking at them. In that case, you are probably going to come up with short cuts and rules of thumb to help you make the decision. Maybe you will think, *Well, if they have a beard, they must be over 18. If they are quite tall, they must be over 18.* You are going to end up thinking in quite a discontinuous way, even though the phenomenon you are dealing with is continuous. The footballing equivalent is decisions about fouls. The absence of an underlying measurement forces us into the tyranny of the discontinuous mind.

We can extend the analogy further. Perhaps the supermarket you work for will try to help you by publishing a rule book with a list of top tips for working out who is over 18 and who is under.

And perhaps every time someone makes a wildly inaccurate decision, they will revise the rules and republish the rule book.

Perhaps they will install CCTV to monitor each of your judgements, and notify you when it looks like you might have made a clear and obvious error, and maybe you will review those judgements and change your mind, but then it will turn out your original decision was actually the right one, and a panel of managers will meet the next day to explain why your original decision was, in fact, correct.

These are not solutions. What we need is a measurement of the underlying continuum. Once we have that, we can easily choose the cut-off score and sort the continuum into two categories.

If we apply this solution to fouls in football, we would need to step back from the game situation and spend some time developing a metric for the underlying continuum. Once we had that, then we could decide where the cut-off line should go – that is, at what point on the continuum an incident becomes a foul.

DESIGNING NEW MEASUREMENTS

Would it be possible to create a measurement for fouls? There are a few interesting recent examples of attempts to measure fairly nebulous concepts. These new measurements are not as precise as those of time and distance, but they can still serve a useful purpose. Risk is a good example. At the start I quoted Dawkins talking about how safety and risk are continuous, and statisticians have helped improve our understanding of risk by developing the 'micromort': a unit of risk equivalent to a one-in-a-million chance of death. Airplane travel is about one micromort per 1,000 miles; riding a motorcycle is one micromort per six miles; running a marathon is seven micromorts, and so on.

A more controversial example is the Quality-Adjusted Life Year, or QALYS, which was developed by health economists as a way to measure the value of new drugs and other medical interventions in terms of the quality of life they provide. For example, perhaps a new drug gives patients an average of ten extra years of life in perfect health. Another might give them an extra 15 years, but their quality of life would be low, perhaps just 25% that of full health. The first drug should get priority for funding.

Sport already has some metrics like these. One popular new football metric is xG, or expected goals, which predicts the likelihood that a particular goal-scoring chance will lead to a goal. Penalty kicks tend to have xGs of about

0.75–0.8, because penalties are scored about 75–80% of the time; long-range shots from the halfway line have xGs of about 0.01.

New metrics like these are not always popular. They reek of the technocratic and the bureaucratic. They are often quite complicated, and it can be difficult for an ordinary person to understand how they produce their judgements. QALYS, in particular, has come in for a lot of criticism for being a devious way of denying people life-saving medicine. When it was first developed, xG was derided as nerdy and misleading, although it does seem to have become more popular over time.

Given that one of the major problems with VAR is the sense of disconnection it has produced between fans and the game, the risk is that any attempt to create a metric for fouls would simply exacerbate this disconnect and be seen as yet another clunky, top-down imposition. For a metric to be accepted, it would need to be easily understood and ideally have an element of fan, player and manager participation. In the next chapter, we will look at how it might work.

7

MEASURING FOULS

'A large acquaintance with particulars often makes us wiser than
the possession of abstract formulas, however deep.'

William James

THE FOUL PROBABILITY INDEX

At its simplest, a metric for fouls could be similar to the
expected-goal metric (xG). xG gives you the percentage
probability that a chance will lead to a goal. A foul metric
– let's call it a Foul Probability Index – could give you the
percentage probability that a particular incident is a foul.

The metric I am proposing would have a crucial difference to xG. xG is a descriptive statistic. It's based on
analysing previous matches and working out the features
of chances that were scored. You could design something exactly the same for fouls. It could analyse previous

matches and work out the features of incidents that referees decided were fouls.But I think we'd be better off not
with a descriptive statistic, but a normative one. A descriptive statistic would tell us if an incident *did* lead to a foul. A
normative one tells us if an incident *should* lead to a foul.

If we go with a descriptive statistic like xG, we will just end
up reproducing the results of laws that we don't necessarily
think are right. But if we go with a normative one, we can
end up with results that reflect what we want the law to be.

This will affect how we create the metric. xG is created by
a team of analysts who go through lots of video clips of goal
chances and break them down according to distance from
goal, angle, proximity to defender, etc. The Foul Probability
Index would also need lots of video clips of possible foul
incidents. But instead of asking a small team of analysts to
categorise them using a list of rules, we should approach
things differently. Here are the three principles we should
use in order to create the metric: first, we should not use a
rule book; second, we should get a large group of referees,
players, managers and fans to judge each video clip; third,
their judgements should be comparative, not absolute.

PRINCIPLE ONE: ELIMINATE THE RULE BOOK

We saw in Chapter 1 that attempts to define handball
precisely in words have caused more problems than they

have solved. These laws have created absurdities, like players trying to run and jump with their hands behind their backs. But they haven't created consistency, because words and phrases like 'immediately', 'some distance' and 'goal-scoring opportunity' are capable of being interpreted in different ways by different people.

If we kept the current laws for our Foul Probability Index, we wouldn't be able to solve this problem. You often hear commentators and ex-players saying things like, 'I don't think that is a foul, but according to the letter of the law, it is.' We want to create a metric that allows the judges to say what they really think a foul should be, not one that forces them to abandon common sense.

So should we try to refine or rewrite the laws? No. The reason why the frequent attempts to rewrite the laws have failed so badly is not because of a lack of effort or skill. It's because language is not well equipped to solve this problem. Plenty of scientists have wrestled with the problem of words not always being as good at communicating meaning as we assume. Scientific concepts like energy, force and the elements have specific meanings that are hard to define in words. If you memorise a definition of 'energy', does that mean you understand the concept?

The philosophers of science Michael Polanyi and Thomas Kuhn have written extensively on this issue. In one essay, Kuhn discusses the challenges of trying to teach these abstract concepts:

Students of physics regularly report that they have read through a chapter of their text, understood it perfectly, but nonetheless had difficulty solving the problems at the end of the chapter. Almost invariably their difficulty is in setting up the appropriate equations, in relating the words and examples given in the text to the particular problems they are asked to solve.[15]

For Kuhn, the solution to this problem is not textbooks that are better written or words that have more precise definitions. For him, the solution is the 'problem set', or the series of exercises at the end of each chapter.

In the course of their training a vast number of such exercises are set for them, and students entering the same specialty regularly do very nearly the same ones . . . These concrete problems with their solutions are what I previously referred to as exemplars, a community's standard examples . . . Acquiring an arsenal of exemplars . . . is integral to the process by which a student gains access to the cognitive achievements of his disciplinary group. Without exemplars he would never learn much of what the group knows about such fundamental concepts as force and field, element and compound, or nucleus and cell. [16]

Complex concepts such as 'force', 'element' and

'compound' are not actually given meaning through prose definitions. Instead, they are defined through 'an arsenal of exemplars' that create a shared meaning that all the members of a particular community agree on, even if they find it hard to put that agreement into words.

Polanyi came up with a term for this hard-to-describe shared understanding: 'tacit knowledge'. There are things we know and can do that we nevertheless find hard to explain in words. Experienced firefighters often know when a building is about to collapse. A carpenter can tell the quality and age of a piece of wood by feeling it. Polanyi's famous phrase is that 'we know more than we can tell'. Our understanding is not always created by language nor capable of being communicated by it. I'd argue that football fans, players, managers and officials all share a kind of tacit knowledge about what is and what isn't a foul. So why not get rid of the rule book and just ask people to give their opinion on whether something should be a foul or not?

The obvious objection to this is the one I put forward in Chapter 1 about the weaknesses of discretionary 'spirit of the law' judgements. The concepts of tacit knowledge and the spirit of the law are similar, and they have the same flaws of inconsistency and subjectivity. The fact that it is so difficult to communicate tacit knowledge is a problem, because it makes it hard to tell the difference between a genuine expert firefighter who really does know when a building is about to collapse and a total charlatan who is just pretending. Since

Chapter 1, I have also put forward a lot more evidence about how even experts are prone to errors and oversights.

What we need is a way of capturing the genuinely powerful insights of tacit knowledge, while filtering out the errors and inconsistencies. Here are two methods that would help.

PRINCIPLE TWO: THE WISDOM OF CROWDS

As we've seen throughout this book, individual humans, even experienced and expert ones, are often error-prone and inconsistent in their judgements. Fortunately, there is a relatively straightforward way around this problem, which is to get more humans involved. When you aggregate human decisions, the inconsistencies and errors cancel each other out.

In the 19th century, the scientist Francis Galton noticed that averaging the judgements of a crowd of people is often better than trusting the judgement of any one of them, however well informed and expert they may be. Galton's famous example of this was a competition at a livestock fair. The villagers were invited to guess the weight of a slaughtered ox. Over 800 took part, and the average of their guesses was almost exactly the same as the actual weight of the animal. Nowadays, a more vegetarian example is to guess the number of sweets in a large jar. You can try it yourself: even if you have only a quite small group of people, the average of their guesses will typically be closer to the actual number than any one individual's guess.

This principle can be applied in lots of weird and

wonderful ways. On the quiz show *Who Wants to Be a Millionaire?*, contestants can choose to ask the audience if they are stuck on a question. The audience's answer is right approximately 90% of the time.

The internet has made it much easier to harness the wisdom of crowds and given plenty of new examples of how powerful that wisdom can be. Wikipedia is a crowd-sourced encyclopaedia that is often more accurate than traditional ones, while open-source software like Linux is robust and secure.

But perhaps the two most significant examples of the wisdom of crowds are in the ways we organise our politics and economics: democracy and stock markets. In a stock market, no one expert sets the price; in a democracy, no one expert picks the prime minister or president. They are both decentralised, distributed systems that are capable of integrating millions of different opinions.

Of course, sometimes crowds of people make bad decisions too, and we have a word for this phenomenon: 'groupthink'. Groupthink happens when views that dissent from the mainstream are suppressed, and it explains an important precondition for the wisdom of crowds to work: every individual judgement must be independent.

To go back to the sweets-in-a-jar example: if, when you are making your guess, you know the guesses of others around you, then it will probably sway your decision. For the wisdom of crowds to succeed, individuals cannot outsource their reasoning to someone else or start 'herding' and copying the guesses of high-status individuals. What is needed instead are lots and lots of independent decisions. The decisions will contain errors, but when you combine them all, the errors cancel each other out.

So, if we want to create a Foul Probability Index, what kind of crowd should we recruit to make the decisions? We could get a large group of expert, experienced referees. But we could, if we wanted, expand the crowd further. We could get players, managers and fans involved as well. Once we have all their decisions, we could analyse the results by type of judge, and if we want to, exclude or include certain groups. It would be interesting and useful to compare the decisions of referees with those of managers, say, and see if the two groups actually agree.

Of course, you can't have players and fans involved in live decision-making because of the risk of bias. But here we are talking about making decisions while watching video clips of incidents taken from matches that have already been completed. To further reduce the risk of bias, you could take the clips from a competition organised specifically for the purpose of making these decisions, something we will look at more in Chapter 11.

PRINCIPLE THREE: COMPARATIVE, NOT ABSOLUTE, JUDGEMENT

One final way we could improve decisions is to use comparative judgements rather than absolute ones.

Absolute judgements are ones where you place an item onto an absolute scale. For example, suppose someone walks into a room, and I ask you how tall they are. Or you put your hand in a basin of water, and I ask you what the temperature is. Those are absolute judgements.

The problem with them is that humans are incredibly bad at them. This is not just true of making judgements about fouls in football, but of making judgements about all kinds of phenomena – height, colour, pitch, temperature, etc.

Our minds hunger for context, for some kind of background information that will help us make a decision. When this context is chosen well, it can help us make better decisions, but when it is chosen badly, we end up making worse ones.

A famous example from a 1968 paper shows how difficult we find absolute judgements. The researchers asked participants to judge a series of actions. They had to place each one on an absolute scale of 1 to 10, where 1 is not that bad and 10 is awful.

(1) Stealing a towel from a hotel
(2) Keeping a dime you find on the ground
(3) Poisoning a barking dog

A second group were asked to do the same, but they

were given the following three actions to judge:

(1*) Testifying falsely for pay
(2*) Using guns on striking workers
(3*) Poisoning a barking dog

Items 3 and 3* are identical, and yet the two groups consistently differed on how they rated them. The second group judged the action to be less evil than those in the first. The reason is not hard to see: when you are thinking in terms of stealing towels and dimes, poisoning a barking dog seems heinous, but in the context of killing humans, it seems less so. Although the participants were asked to judge each item absolutely, on a scale from 1 to 10, they were heavily influenced by the items that came before.

There is nothing wrong with wanting some context for our judgements. What we need to do is set up a means of making them that allows us to use context in a way that doesn't lead to bias and inconsistency. Instead of asking people to place items on an absolute scale, ask them to make comparisons instead. Our brains find them much easier than absolute judgements, and we generally get them right too. Instead of asking them how tall someone is, ask them to look at two people and say who is taller. Instead of asking how dark a shade of purple is on a scale of 1 to 8, show people two shades of purple and ask them which is darker. Instead of asking people how morally bad an action is on a scale of 1 to 10, give them two actions and ask them which is worse.

'OK,' you might say, 'but what we want is an absolute scale. How are all these comparisons going to help us create a scale like the Foul Probability Index?' That is where the comparative judgement technique comes in. It uses exemplification, aggregation and comparison to create meaningful and consistent measurements of apparently subjective concepts.

COMPARATIVE JUDGEMENT

The theory behind comparative judgement was first developed in the 1920s by an American psychometrician, Louis Thurstone.

First, you get a set of exemplars of whatever you want to judge – pictures of shades of purple, audio recordings of songs, student essays, videos of fouls, etc. That's the exemplification principle: you are using exemplars, not definitions or rules.

Second, you ask people to make comparisons between pairs of them, based on just one criterion. For example, if you are comparing colours, your question might be: which colour is darker? If you are comparing moral acts, your question might be: which action is morally worse? If you are comparing songs, your question might be: which song is better? If you are comparing student essays, your question might be: which is the better essay? If you are comparing video clips of fouls, your question might be: which incident is more of a foul? That's the comparison principle.

Third, you get many judges to make a lot of these comparative judgements. That's the aggregation principle.

The comparative judgement algorithm developed by Thurstone then allows you to combine all the judgements together to create a measurement scale that will feature every exemplar. So, taking football as our example, at the end of the process every video clip would have a score, where $1 = $ not a foul and $100 = $ definitely a foul. That's the Foul Probability Index.

Then you would have to decide on various cut-offs: what score on the index is a foul, what score is a yellow card and what score is a red card. There are a couple of different ways of doing this: you could extend the aggregation principle by getting a large group of players, fans, managers and referees to vote on where the thresholds should be; or you could say that this is one place where you need more expert authority, and you could get a panel of referees to decide. Either way, it will be a far more transparent process than what we have currently.

Comparative judgement works. Thurstone's algorithm has been applied successfully in a number of different fields and is particularly valuable for student assessment. At the organisation I work for, we have used it to assess over two million pieces of student writing. The big national exam boards in England use it to maintain assessment standards over time. It's a method of capturing and communicating common sense.

HOW WOULD YOU USE THIS IN A LIVE MATCH?

Even if the Foul Probability Index was never used to make decisions in a live match, it would still be valuable. We'd be able to see if there are big divergences between the judgements of different groups. We'd find out whether fans, players, referees or managers do want marginal handballs to result in penalties. We could identify the incidents that provoked the most disagreement, and those that provoked the least. We'd be able to use the judgements to guide future revisions of the laws and the training of referees.

If we did want to use the Foul Probability Index for making decisions in a live match, we'd need to develop some extra technology. Artificial intelligence is good at pattern recognition, so the next step would be to train an AI model on the Foul Probability Index, and then, in a live match, upload a video clip of an incident from the game to it. The model would decide which clip from the Index it most resembles, and therefore what score it deserves.

The best outcome we could hope for is that the Foul Probability Index would reduce measurement error, add transparency to the decision-making process and allow fans to be involved and give their opinion.

However, such an approach could never completely eliminate measurement error, and nor is it likely it would reduce it down to the tolerances of the goal-line technology. And as we saw in the previous chapter, when you apply a cut-off point to a continuum that has measurement error, it can generate controversy. In the next chapter, we will look at measurement error in more detail, in the context of offside.

8

MARGINS OF ERROR

'Life's single lesson: that there is more accident to it than a man
can ever admit to in a lifetime and stay sane.'

Thomas Pynchon, V.

MEASUREMENT ERROR

In Chapter 3, we saw how fans accept technology making
close goal-line calls, but are much more sceptical of it
deciding on close offside calls. This may partly be because
there is greater measurement error in offsides than in goal-
line decisions.

One response to measurement error is to call for the
introduction of a margin of error, or 'a grey area', which
represents the uncertainty we have about the measurement. This seems like an obvious solution, but in reality it just kicks the can down the road. You can create a

margin of error, sure. But wherever you decide to draw that margin, you will end up with players who will still be deemed to be fractionally beyond it. You could have a margin of error that is plus or minus a foot – and someone would still end up being deemed either offside or onside by a toenail.

There is a close parallel here with exams, which have quite significant measurement error. Imagine an exam that is marked out of 100, but where there is a measurement error of ±10. This means that a pupil getting 90 might actually have scored anywhere between 80 and 100. When people hear this, they often say that you should then create grade boundaries that are at least 20 marks wide, to take account of the measurement error. So, in this case, they would say that the top grade should be awarded to pupils scoring between 80 and 100.

But this does not eliminate the close call, nor does it solve the measurement error problem. Yes, the grade is now 20 marks wide. But the difference between an A and a B is still just one mark! So you will still have essentially indistinguishable candidates getting different grades. This would be true even in a world with no measurement error.

Second, because the boundary is still one mark, it is much smaller than the measurement error, so you will continue to have inconsistencies. You will have a student who scores 79 and gets a B, and one who gets 80 and receives an A. The B-student may have got the wrong end of the error and actually deserve a mark of 89. The A-student may have profited from it and actually deserve a score of just 70.

With exams, this rapidly becomes very technical. People have literally written PhDs on classification accuracy, as it is known. The founder of the company I work for is one of them. Much of this work is devoted to finding the optimal size of a grade for different qualifications. You can have narrow grades that will end up delivering better classification accuracy than much wider ones. But aside from all of the technical details, the major point to note is that if you have a measurement error problem, then a margin of error is not going to cure it. And even if you can eliminate or reduce your measurement error, you will never eradicate the close call.

We can see this with an analogy to speed cameras. Suppose it is true that they are accurate only to within three miles an hour either way. That is, someone measured doing 30 mph might actually be doing anywhere between 27 and 33 mph. Suppose, as a result of this imprecision, lawmakers decide that they will only prosecute people whose speed goes above 33 mph. What will happen? We will still have close calls: people will continue to be penalised for driving just a fraction above 33 mph, and others whose speed is just a fraction lower will not be. You won't have solved the inconsistency problem either. Someone who is actually driving at 31 mph might be measured at 34 mph and fined. Someone going at 34 mph might be measured at 31 mph and not fined.

WHO DOES THE MARGIN OF ERROR BELONG TO?

This speed-camera analogy also shows that introducing a margin of error creates another big problem: who does the margin belong to? In the speed-camera example, lawmakers decide that they will only fine drivers measured at going over 33 mph. What will happen? The average speed of cars on the road will go up as many drivers realise they are unlikely to be fined for drifting above the 30 mph mark. If the legislators decided to go the other way and say that the risk of speeding is so great that they will fine anyone measured at going above 27 mph, then the average speed of cars on the road would go down, as most drivers would limit their speed to 27 mph. Not only that, but you will then just have another set of measurement errors around the new cut-off. If you prosecute anyone measured at above 27 mph, then you will certainly catch everyone going over 30 mph. But the price you will pay for that is to catch a lot of people going at between 24 and 27 mph too. Likewise, if you put the limit up to 33 mph, you will prevent the problem of penalising people who were only going at 27 mph. But the trade-off is that some people will be able to drive at 36 mph and get away with it.

The same will be true of offside. If we introduce a margin for error and say that anyone within it is onside, it will mean we have essentially just rewritten the law in favour of the attackers. If we say that anyone within the margin for error is offside, we have essentially just rewritten it in favour of the defenders.

There is another option: have a margin for error that belongs to the original decision. What this means is that the on-field officials make a decision based on their judgement. VAR reviews it. If it is within the margin of error, the decision is whatever the on-field verdict was. This is exactly the same process that is used in cricket for leg-before-wicket decisions, where it is termed the 'umpire's call' and broadly seems to work well. However, as noted above, it absolutely does not get rid of the close call, because a line still has to be drawn between out and not out. So again, if this system were applied to football, we would still end up scrutinising whether someone's armpit was beyond a certain line.

The other issue with the margin of error belonging to the original decision is that you are guaranteeing inconsistency. Imagine two essentially identical offside incidents. The on-field official calls the first incident as offside, and the second as onside. If, when they are reviewed, both decisions are found to be within the margin of error, then one will remain offside and one onside. Indeed, it can be worse than that: if you have quite a large margin for error, then a decision that looks offside on a replay may remain onside, whereas one that looks onside can remain offside. If a team ended up the wrong side of two such decisions, it is not hard to see how they would feel aggrieved – particularly if, in both cases, it took several minutes to arrive at the decision. Partly because of this issue, cricket's authorities recently decided to reduce the margin of error on leg-be-fore-wicket decisions.

When people talk about a margin for error, what they may actually mean is not that they want one, but that they think the law is too harsh. In Chapter 3, I quoted Roy Hodgson as saying the following:

> That's where we are with VAR, and as a result, we get the situation where people are becoming a bit disillusioned because they're seeing good goals chalked off by very small margins of space, if you like.Hodgson's issue here is less about a margin of error, and more that he thinks that the law is too harsh.

We can fix that without resorting to the minefield that is margins of error. You could change the law so that to be offside, you have to be a certain small distance – maybe half a centimetre – in front of the last defender. This would not eliminate the close call, nor would it eliminate the prob-lem of measurement error: you would still have goals that seemed good being chalked off, and others that seemed off-side being given.

But this change might actually deliver the underlying desire of many of the people who complain about the current law. It would favour the attacking side and would probably mean more goals were scored. In practice, it would effectively restore the pre-VAR offside interpretation, where the benefit of the doubt was given to the attacker.

WHY MEASUREMENT ERROR MATTERS MORE IN FOOTBALL

However, even if we made the offside law a bit more favourable to the attacking team, it would not eliminate all the difficulties with offside decisions. There would still be some measurement error, just as there would be with the Foul Probability Index proposed in the previous chapter. And when you apply cut-offs to continuums that have measurement error, you are always going to have problems. That's because you have to draw a hard and fast cut-off line right through an area where you know for a fact there are no hard and fast certainties.

When people talk about the 'grey areas' involved in close offside decisions and fifty–fifty fouls, they are right to identify that there are some incidents where measurement error means that we cannot be certain which side of the cut-off line the incident lies.

But they are wrong to think that in the case of football, this insight provides us with any practical help. In football, you can award a goal or not. You can't award half a goal or a fraction of a goal. Yes, there are grey zones in football, but there are none in football's scoring system. When you have an incident that lands squarely in that grey zone, you have to make a decision one way or the other.

This is a problem all sports have to grapple with, but it is particularly acute in football because goals are so hard to score and are, relatively speaking, quite rare. Over the last couple of decades in the Premier League, the most common scorelines are 1–1 or 1–0, and over the last ten seasons, the average number of goals per game is 2.8.

Other sports are different. Even the shortest cricket matches will typically feature hundreds of runs and several wickets. There are nearly six tries scored on average in rugby matches in England's Premiership, as well as points scored from penalties. In tennis, a best-of-three-sets match will have a minimum of 48 points. You can have crucial points, tries and wickets in these sports, of course, but when you are reviewing a match, that crucial point, try or wicket will not be the only point, try or wicket.

You can, therefore, take the view that across one match, the problems to do with measurement error will probably even themselves out: yes, that marginal fifty–fifty decision went against you on that point, but you got one in your favour in the next set, so it's all fine. But with football, in most matches teams will be lucky to score a single goal. Goals are precious, precious commodities.

If you were designing a sport from scratch on a piece of paper, and your mission was to make it as entertaining as possible, you might think the best possible plan would be to have lots and lots of scores. If goals and tries and points and wickets are happening all the time, that sounds like it will be fun and entertaining and will capture people's attention.

But it is football that is the world's most popular sport and one of its most popular pastimes. Maybe it achieved this popularity despite its scoring system, but it seems more likely that the scoring system helped cause its popularity.

When you have fewer scores, each one is more important, more memorable and more meaningful. Fewer scores mean more dramatic celebrations. Fewer scores mean that matches are closer; even when one team is superior, the scoreline can be close, and the losing team can feel like they still have a chance. Fewer scores mean the results of individual games are less predictable. A team from a lower league can be outplayed by a team from a higher one but still win if they defend well and take their chances.

Essentially, having fewer scores raises the stakes around each one. This is great for creating an exciting game and is a factor in football's global popularity, but it also means that the refereeing decisions have raised stakes too.

Football's scoring system works well and is not controversial, but fans do recognise its bluntness and are interested in more continuous statistics that give you a sense of the balance of play. Percentage possession, percentage of time spent in the opposition's half, number of corners and number of touches in the opposition's box are examples of relatively straightforward statistics that give you a more continuous sense of which team is playing well, even if the match is goalless.

Now we also have expected goals, a more complicated statistic that indicates the probability of a shot on target leading to a goal. You can aggregate the expected goals to give you an alternative score for a match: maybe your team actually lost 1–0, but on expected goals they won 2.57–0.34. This would suggest a few possibilities: your team were unable to score from some good chances; they had a lot of half chances but were unable to convert any of them; the other team's keeper made some excellent saves; your team's defence did not have a great day; or the other team scored a fantastic goal.

All these statistics can be interesting and insightful, but that's all they are: insightful statistics. They are not the scoring mechanism used in football. If they were, the game might be fairer, but it would not be football any more.

Football has a brutally tough scoring system that makes it hard to translate superiority into scores. That means that refereeing decisions have higher stakes and that decisions with significant measurement error will cause more controversy. We should try to reduce measurement error as much as we can, but there is always going to be some, and it's going to cause more problems in football than in other sports.

WHAT ABOUT SPEED?

Reducing measurement error and drawing the offside line in a way that encourages attacking football is important. However, we saw in Chapter 4 that the problems with the VAR offside system aren't just about making the right decisions, but also how long it takes to make them. The way to solve the latter isn't to ask the referees to hurry up, but to see if there is a way of using technology to make offside decisions in real time, rather than via a retrospective review. We will see how possible that is in the next chapter.

9

AUTOMATION

Some day there will be machines of the heart that
   will not wear out,
Machines with a soul, imperturbable to any suffering,
And the people, who use them, will themselves
   become machines, soulless and eternal.

Rainer Maria Rilke

HUMAN REVIEW VS TECHNOLOGICAL REVIEW

Let's imagine it's 1975, and you want a small loan from the bank to do a few home improvements. You go to the bank, talk to the manager, answer a few questions and then a few days later get a letter from the manager with his decision: no, you can't have the loan. This is a system of human judgement.

Let's imagine that it's 1980, and you want a small loan from the bank to do a few home improvements. You go to the bank, talk to the manager, answer a few questions and then a few days later get a decision: no, you can't have the loan. You're pretty unhappy about this. A friend of yours in similar financial circumstances got an equivalent loan from the same bank just a few weeks earlier. You ask the bank if there is any kind of appeal process. Yes, they say. We have this amazing new technology called a fax machine. We can fax your application over to the manager of a neighbouring branch, and he can review your application and see if we have made the right decision. This is a system of human judgement with human review.

Let's imagine it's 1985, and you want a small loan from the bank to do a few home improvements. You go to the bank, and the manager has this newfangled computer sitting on his desk. You talk to him, and he doesn't look at you; he just types what you are saying into the computer. When you've finished answering all his questions, the computer tells him no, do not give this person a loan. But he doesn't tell you that. He says, 'We'll let you know in a couple of days.' This is a semi-automated system of judgement.

Let's imagine it's 2015, and you want a small loan from the bank to do a few home improvements. You go online, answer a few questions and get an immediate answer. No, you can't have a loan. This is fully automated judgement.

The way technology is used in football at the moment is a mish-mash of the first three approaches. Many decisions are made by a human referee and are not subject to any kind of review. Some get reviewed by other humans and/or the referee. Goal-line decisions are the closest to being fully automated, but they are still not completely. IFAB make it clear that goal-line technology is there to support referees, not to replace them. The decision made by the GLT is sent to the referee, who retains final responsibility for signalling whether or not there has been a goal and stopping play, if necessary. A fully automated system would give the power of stopping play to the GLT. Offside is also moving further along the automation continuum, from a human review system to a semi-automated system that is more like GLT.

Tennis provides an example of full automation. Computer-vision technology was first introduced there in 2006, but only as part of a player challenge system. All decisions were made by the on-court line judges, and players were given two opportunities to challenge those decisions. By 2020, line technology had completely replaced human line judges in some tournaments, making instant decisions about whether the ball was in or out.

For all the talk of technology in football, many aspects of its use are remarkably basic. VAR doesn't use technology to make decisions, but to facilitate human review, which is about as pioneering as using a fax machine to review a loan application. And, as we saw in the previous chapter, adding more human review often just adds more problems. We're not using technology to mitigate human weaknesses or complement our strengths. We're using it to multiply the opportunities for human error.

THE ADVANTAGE OF SPEED

If you can automate a process, the enormous advantage is speed. In many different sectors, this more than makes up for the drawbacks of automation. When banks are approving small loans or credit lines, human decisions might in some ways be better than automated algorithmic ones, but those benefits are offset by the fact that by comparison, they are slow and expensive. The marginal benefits they might bring are just not worth it.

If we could automate some of the decisions in football, it would solve a lot of problems. As we saw in Chapter 4, some of the issues with VAR concern not its accuracy, but the time it takes to make a decision and the way that gums up the traditional flow of the game.

The quickest, most automated aspect of football decision-making is goal-line technology, which is also the most successful. The referee is sent a message about whether the ball has crossed the line or not straight away.

The obvious next step would be to try and automate offside, which is also a line call. A few tournaments over the past few years have trialled semi-automated offside, and the Premier League will be introducing it in 2024–25.

Such systems draw the offside lines automatically, which would eliminate the human error issues we saw in Chapter 5. They also track all the players using specially calibrated cameras, and in some versions, identify the exact moment a player touches the ball, using information from a sensor inside it. The system can then automatically tell the video assistant referee if any players are offside. The VAR then has to manually review the incident to see if the offside player is interfering with play.

In the competitions where it has been used, it has seemed like a definite improvement on the manual system. However, there are still caveats. There are concerns that its greater precision might create more of the incredibly marginal offside calls that people dislike about the manual system. Perhaps if the decisions are arrived at quickly and there is more faith in the underlying measurement, those decisions will be less annoying. Or perhaps not – we will have to see.

And it can still take its time in arriving at a decision. Olympiakos's winner in the 2024 Europa Conference League final took a while to be confirmed by the semi-automated system in use in that game. Even if the technology could be sped up, it's unlikely that it could, on its own, develop into a completely automated system because of the two subjective elements of offside, which currently need human review. So the problem of the late flag will remain.

Automating subjective decisions in real time is the

hardest problem of all. I set out a possible way of doing so in Chapter 7, but it would need a lot of research and testing to see if it was feasible. In the short term, if we are to permit reviews of subjective decisions, they will not be automated and will have to be managed by humans. But which humans? Currently, the review process is managed entirely by the officials. But in other sports, players have a say in deciding what will and won't be reviewed. Would it be worth football thinking about such a player challenge system? We will consider that in the next chapter.

10

AUTONOMY

Ah, but a man's reach should exceed his grasp,
Or what's a heaven for?

Robert Browning

PLAYER REVIEW SYSTEMS

Cricket is a sport with a reputation for conservatism and tradition that is not always deserved. It has pioneered some of the most interesting uses of technology in sport, and it is worth exploring how they work in more detail.

In 1992, cricket introduced a third umpire, who could watch a slow-motion TV replay to help decide on run-outs. This may not seem like a particularly astounding innovation, but it took football 25 years to use technology for equivalent line decisions. In 2008, the International Cricket Council introduced a much more sophisticated Decision

Review System (DRS), which is generally well regarded and is now an established part of the game at elite level.

The impetus behind its introduction was similar to that of football: to eliminate the glaring error. And the major challenge was similar too: how do you eliminate the glaring error without subjecting every single other decision to scrutiny as well? Football's VAR system responded to this challenge by saying that only certain categories of decision would be eligible for review. It also set a high bar for overturning subjective decisions – the 'clear and obvious' test.

However, while only certain categories were eligible for review, every single incident that belonged to them would be checked in the background by the video assistant referee. In practice, quite a lot of decisions fall into these categories, meaning that the VAR is involved a lot of the time. And as we've seen, the 'clear and obvious' threshold for overturning a decision has turned out to be not nearly as high a bar as was assumed. So, in practice, it does often feel like the game is being re-refereed from a video truck.

Cricket took a different approach. It was decided that the officials would not be in charge of deciding what to review; instead, the players would be. The on-field umpires would continue to make decisions on the field of play, but players could challenge those decisions. However, they could have only two unsuccessful challenges per innings (since increased to three.)

This was a bold call. An important principle in a lot of

sports is that the official's word is final. If you start allowing player challenges, that undermines that principle. Not only that, but if the aim of technology is to get more right decisions, then the official might be better placed to decide what should be reviewed, as they will often have a more comprehensive and unbiased view of what has happened. By contrast, players might use reviews tactically or incompetently, and their main motivation might be not to get more correct decisions, but to get the right decision for them.

For these reasons, not everyone in cricket did support the concept of a player challenge system when it was first proposed, and there are a couple of interesting examples of alternative systems. In 2005, before DRS existed, the ICC trialled a system that was much more like VAR, where the power to review decisions stayed with the umpire. It was used only in a one-off Test match between Australia and a World XI, but even in that one game it led to confusion and was not used again in international matches. In 2012–13, the Australian Cricket Board (ACB) trialled a similar umpire-led review system in Australian domestic cricket. It was an unmitigated disaster that was abandoned mid-season. And many of the problems were exactly the same as those affecting VAR in football. It was confusing, slow and inconsistent. Umpires reviewed decisions that didn't need reviewing. Players didn't know what was going on. One senior player described the system as 'shocking and embarrassing', even after his team benefited from a decision that was overturned on review. One of the administrators responsible for introducing it said, 'When it was talked about conceptually we didn't see the problems that would come up.'[17]

In theory, giving officials the ability to review their decisions feels sensible and straightforward. In practice, it leads to confusion, uncertainty and embarrassment. Ironically, allowing umpires to challenge themselves undermines their authority more than allowing players to do so.DRS is still going strong. It has had its controversial moments, but nothing like VAR or the ACB's system. In fact, until VAR started failing so obviously, it had never even occurred to me to ask whether DRS had been successful or not. It had just become an accepted part of cricket.

However, when you examine DRS more closely, it has more in common with VAR than you might think. Neither DRS nor VAR have eliminated the glaring error, and neither review system is used sparingly. Both have led to enormous unintended consequences and have fundamentally changed the interpretation of crucial laws: offside and handball in football's case, and leg before wicket in cricket. Neither system works as its original proponents said it would. But in cricket, everyone seems OK with what has happened, whereas in football, they aren't. Let's look at some of the unintended consequences in cricket.

DRS IS NOT USED SOLELY FOR GLARING ERRORS

Cricket teams do not reserve their reviews to overturn clear and obvious errors. The most obvious piece of evidence for this is that most fail. Only about a quarter of player reviews are successful, and of those that are, clearly not all are glaring errors. Sometimes a fielding team will burn through their reviews in the first few overs of a match, and then have to toil through the rest of the innings without any.

There are also significant signs that teams use reviews tactically. Senior batters tend to use the reviews for themselves more, and to do so with less success. Fielding teams tend to use the reviews against the other team's star batters. Anecdotally, it feels as if a team that has been toiling in the field for a long time without a wicket is more likely to call for a marginal review than one that is doing well and taking wickets.

DRS HAS NOT ELIMINATED THE GLARING ERROR

You would think that as players are using DRS so much, it would have eliminated the glaring error. But it has not, for two reasons.

First, it turns out that players are not good at umpiring. It isn't just that they ask for reviews of perfectly good decisions. That's easy to predict, and can be at least partly explained by them using the system tactically, as discussed above. What is more surprising is that sometimes they fail to ask for reviews when they should. Perhaps the most surprising thing we've learnt from DRS is that batters do not always know when they have nicked the ball. There have been examples of players not reviewing the decision after edging to the wicketkeeper and being given out. The replay then shows the ball missing the bat. Of course, it could be that the technology has failed in some way, but there is a growing consensus that batters really cannot tell if they have got a very fine edge or not. This is an example of technology turning up something interesting and unexpected about reality – but in this case, it hasn't undermined the game, unlike in football.

Cricket players are no better at determining leg-before-wicket decisions. Perhaps one of the worst umpiring decisions of all time took place in the 2013 Ashes series. Graeme Swann was bowling to Chris Rogers, when the ball slipped out of his hand early and hit Rogers on the pads. Swann appealed, and the umpire gave it out. Rogers looked confused and thought about reviewing, but decided against it. A subsequent projection showed that the ball would have missed the stumps by about six inches. If we judge how bad an error is based on magnitude, this was an extremely big mistake. And yet the batter had the opportunity to review it, and failed to do so. You could argue that it was a strange situation, and it was, because the way the ball slipped out of Swann's hand created an unusual angle. But it is precisely these kinds of odd decisions that technology was supposed to fix.

The second reason why DRS has not eliminated the glaring error is because teams often waste all their reviews on marginal calls, and then have none left when the glaring error does come along.

The two most famous examples also occurred in Ashes Tests, and Australia were again on the wrong side of both. In the 2013 Test at Trent Bridge, Stuart Broad edged the ball and was caught at slip. But the umpire missed the edge and did not give him out. England scored a further 59 runs before Broad was dismissed, and went on to win the match by just 14 runs, so this decision was a crucial moment in the game. Australia were unable to review it, however, because they had already used up all their reviews.

In 2019, something similar occurred in the Headingley Test. Ben Stokes was batting and was just a few runs away from helping his team to complete one of the most famous run chases in cricketing history. Nathan Lyon pinned him in front of his stumps with a delivery that looked like it was out, leg before wicket. The umpire disagreed, saying it was not out. Again, Australia had no reviews left to challenge the decision. What made matters even worse this time was that they had used up their final review on a speculative appeal just a few overs earlier.

DRS HAS CHANGED THE WAY THE LEG-BEFORE-WICKET LAW WORKS

The leg-before-wicket law is similar to football's offside law in that it is a source of constant controversy and has been adjusted incessantly over the years. As with offside, there is a 'spirit' at the heart of the law that is necessary for the game to function. Batters should try to hit the ball with their bats; they shouldn't use their legs to stop it hitting the wicket. But defining that basic principle in a way that cannot be manipulated or exploited has always proven tricky.

Leg before wicket is also a difficult decision for a human to make in real time, so just as with offside, the law acknowledged that some decisions would involve doubt and recommended whom the benefit of the doubt should go to. In cricket, it used to go to the batter. This changed with the introduction of DRS: the benefit of the doubt would instead go to the umpire's original decision.

But the real impact of DRS has gone beyond this law change. For lbw decisions, DRS uses ball-tracking software that predicts whether a ball would go on to hit the stumps. Before DRS, umpires used an informal rule of thumb to help them make lbw decisions: if a spinner was bowling, and a batter made a big stride forward before being hit on the pad, they would be less likely to give them out. Batters knew this, and so they realised that if they made a big stride forward, they could use their pads to play the ball. Once DRS came along, this didn't work any more. If the ball was going on to hit the stumps, ball-tracking software would tell you, regardless of whether the batter had taken a stride or not.

So, we were told at the beginning that DRS would be used sparingly, with the aim of overturning bad decisions, and that it would have little impact on the way the game was played. In practice, it is used a lot, has not eliminated the bad decision and has changed the interpretation of one of cricket's most fundamental laws.

These are the unintended consequences that critics of DRS feared. And yet, as I said at the start of this chapter, it seems as though DRS has worked. We don't get fans and players regularly lining up to pour scorn on the system. Why is this?

The changes in the way the lbw law is interpreted are generally considered to have been positive. They have made it easier for off-spin bowlers, in particular, to take wickets, by stopping batters from employing the fairly cynical tactic of striding down the wicket but not attempting to play the ball with their bat. The change has been in keeping with the spirit of the lbw law, not opposed to it.

But another interesting reason why DRS has been successful is that people aren't interested only in getting the right decision. Other things matter too, and what we are realising from cricket is that one of those things is autonomy. If a team fail to review a glaring error because they decide against it or have already used up their reviews, then they have no one to blame but themselves. A system has been deliberately put in place to help guard against such unfairnesses, and they have misused it. It was striking that after umpire Joel Wilson's lbw decision in the Headingley Test, the Australian media queued up to heap abuse not on his head, but on their captain's, for having blown his last review a few overs earlier.

There is a useful concept in political science that can shed some light on what is happening here. In any system, you have process legitimacy and outcome legitimacy. Outcome legitimacy is about getting the right decision. Process legitimacy is about having the right process.

In a dream world, if we followed the right process, we would get the right decision. We might want to believe that, and in many cases it might well be true. There is plenty of evidence that democracy leads to better outcomes than autocracy, that enforcing property rights leads to wealthier societies and that societies with the rule of law are more peaceful than those without it.

However, it also clear that people's attachment to democracy and the rule of law is deeper than whether they lead to the right decision or not. We can probably all think of plenty of examples where democracy has led to the wrong outcome, but we accept it because we are committed to the process.

I think something similar is happening with cricket. The new player challenge system creates a fairer process, even if it doesn't guarantee the right outcomes. Of course, you can't push this too far. A process that routinely leads to bad outcomes will start to be questioned, even if it has the surface features of fairness. It's a trade-off: we are probably never going to eliminate every bad decision, but certain processes make them more or less tolerable.So should football introduce a player challenge system? The traditional argument against this is that football doesn't have the same natural breaks in play as cricket. In cricket, teams have fifteen seconds from the umpire's original decision in which to launch a review. In football, it would be much harder to determine such a window, and it would be much more open to being gamed by teams. The most sensible approach would probably be for a manager to call for a review within 15 seconds of the incident occurring, but for play to continue until the next time the ball went out. You'd still have the ghost-minute and the 'clear and obvious' problems, but it would stop large chunks of the game being re-refereed from a video truck, and would probably cut down the number of interruptions too.

On balance, I still think a player challenge system would be incredibly difficult to implement. But one of the things we have seen again and again with all of the review systems is that it is really hard to predict in advance how they will turn out. Unintended consequences – for good and for ill – are everywhere. So perhaps it would be worthwhile trialling some new systems, as that is the only way we are going to discover if they really work or not. We will look at the importance of transparent trials in the next chapter.

11

TRANSPARENCY

'What is truth?' said jesting Pilate, and would not stay for an answer.'

Francis Bacon

WHAT DO FANS NEED TO KNOW?

One of the major differences between decision reviews in football and in other sports is that in football, the system is far less transparent.

Fans in the ground get little information about the review process; there are no replays of any controversial decisions, whether they are referred to VAR or not. Fans watching at home on TV get to see normal replays and the graphics used to decide offsides, but the discussions between the various different officials are not played live for anyone. In the Premier League in 2023–24, some of these recordings were released after the match was over. In sports like cricket, by contrast, the officials' dialogue is played live and can be heard by fans in the ground too.

One argument in favour of greater transparency in football is that it will provide fans with more clarity about what is going on. The current system is confusing: those in the ground often don't know what's happening, and even if you are watching on TV, there are still long delays while everyone waits for an update.

If fans had greater clarity about how the decisions were made, there might be fewer objections to the decisions themselves, even if everything else stayed the same.

I think there is some truth to this. If VAR had to stay in place in its current form, and I were allowed to make just one change to it, I would let TV replays of VAR incidents be shown on the big screen inside the ground. The suggestion is that the football authorities are reluctant to allow this because it will lead to bad fan behaviour and could undermine the referee or put undue pressure on them. Those are realistic considerations that should be taken seriously, and they're a reason to think carefully about transparency in general, as we shall discuss. But currently, fans in the ground are in the absurd situation of spending lengthy VAR checks texting their friends at home to find out what is going on.

WILL TRANSPARENCY IMPROVE DECISION-MAKING?

However, while more transparency might improve the matchday experience and people's overall opinion of VAR, would it do anything to alleviate some of the fundamental problems with VAR that we've looked at so far? The more far-reaching goal of transparency is to improve decisions, not just publicise them. The argument is that if you release audio of the discussions between officials – either live or after the match – this might actually improve the quality of those discussions and make it more likely that the officials reach the right decision.

How likely is it that greater transparency will lead to better decision-making? This point has been debated in politics and philosophy for centuries. The ancient Greek philosopher Glaucon asked his audience to imagine what might happen if an individual were given the mythical ring of Gyges, which makes its wearer invisible. Would that individual behave impeccably? Or would they get up to all forms of naughtiness, safe in the knowledge they could never be identified or punished? These questions have enormous implications for the design of modern institutions.

The modern social psychologist Philip Tetlock has carried out a number of experiments to try and find the answers. In one, he gave individuals information about a legal case and asked them to make a judgement. Some individuals were told they would have to explain their decision to a group of people, whereas others wouldn't. The group who knew in advance that they would have to explain themselves took more time and considered the evidence more carefully. Those who didn't were lazier and more error-prone.

Generally speaking, the assumption of many researchers is that transparency improves accountability. The Supreme Court justice Oliver Wendell Holmes gave the best description of this second function of transparency when he said that 'sunlight is the best disinfectant'.

A similar debate has played out at the top of the British state. In 1997, the Labour Party won a landslide election victory, and their manifesto promised a Freedom of Information Act that would give the public right of access to information held by public authorities. It was a bold commitment to creating more transparent government. Before the election, the Labour leader, Tony Blair, gave speeches in which he sounded like a committed Glauconian warrior for greater transparency. In 1996, he won an award from the Campaign for Freedom of Information, and in his prize-winning speech he said the following:It is not some isolated constitutional reform that we are proposing with a Freedom of Information Act. It is a change that is absolutely fundamental to how we see politics developing in this country over the next few years . . . information is power and any government's attitude about sharing information with the people actually says a great deal about how it views power itself and how it views the relationship between itself and the people who elected it.

The Freedom of Information Act was eventually passed in 2000, and its various provisions were all implemented by 2005.

But Blair's enthusiasm for transparent information sharing did not last. In his memoirs, published in 2010, three years after stepping down as prime minister, he called his younger self a 'naïve, foolish, irresponsible nincompoop' for passing a law 'so utterly undermining of sensible government'.

It's hard to imagine a more dramatic change of opinion. Pre-1997 Blair thought sunlight was the best disinfectant. Post-2007 Blair thought that sunlight was corrosive to good government.

For freedom-of-information campaigners, Blair's U-turn was entirely predictable, if depressing. Of course politicians are in favour of transparency and openness when they are in opposition and it doesn't affect them. And of course, once they assume power, they loathe transparency and openness because it does affect them. In their reading, power is essentially the ring of Gyges. If you don't have it, naturally you are going to campaign for it to be destroyed. But once you do have the magic ring that makes you invisible, you will suddenly come up with all kinds of specious reasoning for why you should, in fact, retain it. It's the eternal challenge of all attempts to place checks and balances on power: in order to check power, you need power, and the people who have it are often extremely reluctant to place checks on themselves, despite what they might have said beforehand.

Still, even if you are completely cynical about Blair's motivations, it is worthwhile thinking more about the substantive part of his argument. The phrase that's become shorthand for the problems identified by Blair is the 'chilling effect'. When we know that what we say can be revealed to the entire public, does that make us more focused, less error-prone, more likely to make good decisions? Or does it just make us less likely to say anything in the first place?

Imagine this in your own life. If we are being honest, we can probably accept that being given a ring that makes us invisible would not be great for the morality of our actions. But we can probably also see that having every conversation made public might cause other problems. Suppose that your mother-in-law is staying with you after an illness, and you want to have a conversation with your spouse about how long she will be staying. Suppose you are told that the transcript of your conversation will be released to your mother-in-law straight afterwards. Does that make you more focused, less error-prone and more likely to make the right decision? Or does it just make you think that you won't have the conversation at all?

That is Blair's point: knowing that the details of a debate will be made public makes it less likely that the participants

will speak freely and frankly about potentially delicate matters. Civil servants adapt and change the advice they give
to the government for fear of what it will look like if it is
subjected to an FOI request, and everyone in government
finds ways to communicate that are off the record and not
subject to FOI.

This is similar to the problems with slow-motion scrutiny we looked at in Chapter 2. Generally speaking, scrutiny is a good thing that leads to better decision-making.
But as we've seen, when you scrutinise a lot of fouls and
play them back at different speeds and angles, they often
look a lot worse than they really are. The FOI Act is a kind
of political equivalent of the slow-motion replay: when
you use it to request lots of documents, you can pull out
excerpts that make decision-makers look particularly bad.

Blair goes on to argue that this happened a lot.
Transparency was weaponised, and rather than being
used by the public to see how government worked, it was
used by journalists and political opponents to attack the
government. In his words: The truth is that the FOI Act
isn't used, for the most part, by 'the people'. It's used by
journalists. For political leaders, it's like saying to someone
who is hitting you over the head with a stick, 'Hey, try this
instead', and handing them a mallet. The information is
neither sought because the journalist is curious to know,
nor given to bestow knowledge on 'the people'. It's used
as a weapon. These debates also apply to releasing audio

and video footage from VAR. What we need to think about is this: if we introduce more transparency into the VAR process, what do we hope will happen, and what do we not want to happen?

The best-case scenario is that transparency will shine a light on the problems, motivate everyone to pull their socks up and focus people's minds on finding solutions. This is clearly possible, and in a previous chapter we saw one example where it has already happened. Releasing the audio of the Luis Díaz error led to the Premier League realising how poor the VAR protocols were and requesting changes. This is a textbook example of how transparency can help solve a problem. If the protocols for making off-side decisions could be improved and standardised so that they are more like those in rugby and cricket, then it would make sense to release those recordings. To start with, they could be released after the match, and if all went well, they could be broadcast live too.

What do we not want? The worst-case scenario is that fans spend ever more time scrutinising replays of officials' conversations to find examples of bias, disagreement and error. That transparency and scrutiny leads to not improvement, but degradation, as officials' cease to have honest and frank discussions for fear of how they will be misinterpreted. And that there are no solutions, just increasingly toxic disagreements fuelled by increased information. There are signs of this already in the comments on some of the audio that's been released. It's legitimate, therefore, to be cautious about releasing all audio recordings of discussions, and particularly about releasing them live.

LAW LABS

We also need to think about where we want to shine the spotlight. This entire discussion about transparency has essentially looked at decision-making's front line: the discussions between the various officials at the moment a decision is made. But as we saw in Chapter 5, there are so many other, hidden aspects of the system that determine what happens in those high-profile discussions. If we focus on making the live discussions transparent but neglect the processes behind them, we will miss something extremely important. I think we should be more transparent not just with the way the laws are implemented, but with the way they are created. In Chapter 7, I outlined how you could create a more transparent method of measuring fouls. You could combine that method with a transparent, televised system of 'law labs': a league or competition where new laws are trialled, and fans get to see the trials and vote on their impact.

When rugby union turned professional in 1995, it introduced law labs to help with the greater pressure that the laws and lawmakers would face in the new era. One of their creators, Dick Tilley, said that in 1995, 'the professional game had just come in and players and coaches suddenly found themselves thinking about the game 24/7. As a result they started coming up with ways of using and abusing the laws, something which happens in any professional sport.'[18]

The law labs took place in matches between Cambridge University's 24 colleges and allowed referees to see the second-order consequences of new laws. For example, one that was trialled and discarded was a ban on tackling above the waist, because 'players found a way of running while hunched over, making it almost impossible for them to be tackled legally'.[19] As we saw in Chapter 10, it is surprisingly hard to predict the impact of changes to laws and review systems. Unintended consequences are everywhere, and law labs help you identify them.

The ideal competition for a football law lab would be one that was of a sufficiently high standard to provide insights for the elite game, but low stakes enough to allow tinkering. If we wanted to use video clips from this competition to create a Foul Probability Index, then ideally it would involve teams that weren't affiliated to any elite clubs, given the biases that might introduce. Maybe it could be a specially organised summer tournament featuring teams made up of players who have been released from youth academies.

CONCLUSION

To sum up, here's what I'd propose in order to fix VAR:·
Pause VAR immediately.

· Launch a two-year programme of law labs, with three
main aims:

(a) to create a crowdsourced Foul Probability Index;
(b) to test a player review system;
(c) to test a more lenient offside law.· Other innovations
could be tested too, based on feedback from players and
fans.

· Depending on the results of these trials, a reformed
VAR could be reintroduced to professional matches.

These discussions have thrown up some bigger issues
about the possibility of progress and the nature of authority. We'll look at them in the final part.

PART 4
DIVERSIONS

12

PROGRESS

'In order for things to stay the same, they are going to have
to change.'

Giuseppe Tomasi di Lampedusa

SAUSAGES AND LAWS

In the previous chapter on transparency, we saw that
one of the crucial points was whether transparency led
to progress or not. The cynical conclusion is as follows:
systems which are closed and protective of their decision-
making processes generally *do* have something to hide.
If you expose them, you probably *will* find lots of nasty
things. However, it is possible that exposure will not lead to
improvement, because the nasty things might be essential
to the system.

In a political sense, what this means is that all the nasty

things we associate with bad governance and which look so awful when they are exposed are actually essential to getting laws passed in a democracy. The grubby compromises, the patronage, the bribes, the lies, the saying one thing to one group and another thing to another, the broken promises – all these aren't bugs in the system. They are features.

Bismarck gave the clearest summary of the cynic's critique of transparency when he said that there are two things you don't want to see being made: sausages and laws. The best cinematic depiction of this point is in the courtroom drama *A Few Good Men*. Tom Cruise plays Daniel Kaffee, a lawyer trying to uncover the circumstances that led to the death of Santiago, a young Marine. He questions the senior commander, Nathan Jessep, who is at the heart of the cover-up, and asks him to tell the truth. Jessep explodes into a famous monologue, in which he concedes that Santiago was illegally punished, but tells Kaffee that 'you can't handle the truth'.

His argument essentially is that the illegal punishments that led to Santiago's death are a necessary feature of national security. The ordinary person cannot face that truth. They want to pretend that the security they seek and rely on does not require such viciousness. And because the ordinary person cannot handle that truth, the only possibility is to cover it up and hush up the deaths that follow.

If we applied this analysis to football, the 'truth' would be that many of football's laws are essentially impossible to apply accurately, with or without technology, that disagreements are inevitable, and that much of the time it makes no sense even to talk about 'errors', given the impossibility of agreeing on what the actual decisions should be. The ordinary person cannot face that truth. They want to pretend that the laws work and that a flawless decision-making system is possible. And because the ordinary person cannot handle that truth, the only possibility is to cover it up and suppress discussion and scrutiny.

The conclusion of *A Few Good Men* is that Jessep is abusing his power and using the military's culture of secrecy to create a ring of Gyges-style invisibility cloak for himself. The hero is Daniel Kaffee, who thinks that national security and a bully-free military can co-exist. In fact, he'd go further and say that natural security is *improved* by a bully-free military. This is the key point. If you think national security and a bully-free military are not in tension, and indeed may even complement each other, then transparency is a good thing. If you think the opposite, then transparency is a bad thing. Likewise, if you think that football's laws and accurate decision-making are not in tension with each other, then transparency is a good thing.

Transparency is a good pathway towards better outcomes when such an outcome is possible. When it is not possible, for whatever reason, then transparency will focus a lot of attention on the bad outcomes, but it won't help you get to a better one, because that is impossible. In that

I CAN'T STOP THINKING ABOUT VAR

situation, you might have been better off not opting for transparency, as it means you have just focused a lot of attention on problems you cannot fix.

Faith in transparency is, therefore, intimately bound up with faith in progress. If you think progress is possible, transparency is a good way of getting there. If you think it isn't, transparency will only make things worse.

IS PROGRESS POSSIBLE?

To what extent is it possible to make progress with VAR? Is it capable of being improved? One constant response from lots of people is that it works in other sports, so why not football? But as we have seen throughout this book, other sports are different. You can't just copy and paste what they do. The snickometer is a great solution for cricket and a terrible one for football. And when you do start to compare different sports, you realise that football has unique features that make it harder to do reviews. And those features are what make football the most popular sport in the world. It is fluid and fast-moving, with few natural breaks in play and few scores, and it has a passionate, spontaneous fan culture.

People made this argument before VAR was introduced, and it did sound like special pleading. But after four years of VAR controversies, maybe there is something to it.

174

Ultimately, some problems *are* just harder to solve than others.

In Chapter 5, we looked at the way aviation had solved a lot of safety problems by getting humans to use checklists, and in Chapter 9 we looked at how automation, which is also an important part of modern aviation, can reduce the potential for human error. When you compare the safety records of airplanes with those of cars on the road, the difference is stark. In the US, there are 0.01 injuries per 100 million miles of passenger travel by airplane.[20] For cars and trucks, the figure is 48. Cars are simpler and less dangerous than airplanes, yet they end up doing much more damage.

Could you borrow from the world of aviation to try and reduce road fatalities? In some ways, yes. You could view car accidents as part of a system, not as just a result of human error, and change the system to make accidents less likely. You could redesign roads that are accident hot spots, add safety features like airbags and seatbelts to cars, and introduce speed limits and stricter laws around drink driving. In a number of countries, changes like these have made an enormous difference to the safety of car travel. However, it is *still* much more dangerous than going by plane.

What would it take to make cars as safe as planes? Let's consider a few possible policies. You could dramatically raise the competence threshold for getting a driving licence. You could fit cars with immobilisers that prevent them being used by drivers with too much alcohol in their system or who haven't had enough sleep. You could ban all driving on days with particularly bad weather. You could ban driving in residential areas and at accident hot spots. You could set up an advance booking system to limit the number of cars on the road at any one time.

If you did all this, it wouldn't be car travel as we know it any more. The thing people want from a private car is flexibility: the ability to use it whenever they want, wherever they want. The features of car travel that we like are inherently risky. A lot of accidents are hard to prevent without severely curtailing individual car use.

The solution that's been proposed over the past few years is self-driving cars, and on the surface this feels like a brilliant one. It would be unrealistic to enforce the kind of safety protocols airlines have on private drivers, but if you could automate them, that would basically solve the problem. And perhaps at some point self-driving cars will take over. But currently, it is fair to say that autonomous vehicles have hit a few roadblocks, and the roadblocks they have hit are essentially the same ones that make car travel inherently risky. Getting them to work in all weather conditions is hugely challenging. Getting them to work on irregular or unusual residential road layouts is hugely challenging. Getting them to cope with rare incidents, known as 'edge cases', is hugely challenging. But again, all these things are exactly what we want from private car use.

So maybe cricket and tennis are more like air travel, in that their structures are more amenable to automation and the application of technology. Football is more like car travel. It is more fluid and irregular, and that makes it harder for technology to solve its problems.

WHAT ARE THE LIMITS OF PROGRESS?

Racehorses are bred for speed. Over the last few hundred years of selective breeding, they've got faster and faster. Will they keep getting faster and faster? At what point will the benefits of selective breeding level out? Will they never level out? Could racehorses end up travelling faster than Formula One cars? Could they break the sound barrier?

No. When you keep breeding racehorses for speed, you reach a point where their bones get too light and break too easily. Their speed is constrained by bone density. Constraints and trade-offs are everywhere in evolution.

The body is a bundle of trade-offs. Everything could be better, but only at a cost. Your immune system could react more strongly, but at the cost of increased tissue damage. The bones in your wrist could be thick enough that you could safely skateboard without wrist guards, but then your wrist would not rotate and you could throw a rock only half as far. You could have an eagle's ability to spot a mouse from a mile away, but only at the cost of eliminating colour vision and peripheral vision. Your brain could have been bigger, but at the risk of death during birth. Your blood pressure could be lower, at the cost of weaker, slower movement. You could be less sensitive to pain, at the cost of being injured more often. Your stress system could be less responsive, at the cost of coping less well with danger.[21]

There are a lot of trade-offs in other walks of life. Indeed, you can make the argument that all solutions to any problem, technological or otherwise, are not really solutions but trade-offs. Sometimes, it's really obvious that the thing we are trading off is worth it. In other cases, it's not so clear. And you can't trade off endlessly: if you keep optimising racehorses for speed and trading off every other feature to increase it, eventually you get to a point where their bones break and they have zero speed. You'll have given up everything for nothing.

So it is with football. How much progress on accurate decisions is possible within the constraints of the game as it currently exists? What are we willing to give up in order to get more accurate decisions? How much more accurate do those decisions have to be in order to justify what we lose? And at what point do we give up so much that the game's bones break?

When should we try to change things, and when should we decide to preserve them?

13

AUTHORITY

That man's the true conservative,
who lops the mouldered branch away.

Alfred Tennyson

Here are three simplified attitudes to change and preservation:

The liberal says that institutions should always be trying to improve. They need to be self-critical and must constantly look for ways to exercise power in a fairer and more just way. The way to make these improvements is through rational thought. This was the impulse behind the introduction of VAR: refereeing was flawed, and VAR will improve it.

The conservative is wary of change. They want to preserve. They'll argue that total fairness and justice are impossible to achieve, and also that human rationality often fails to anticipate the real-world consequences of change. They will point out that things can *always* get worse. This provides us with the standard critique of VAR: it might have solved some problems, but it has left us with a whole set of new ones, and the game is no fairer as a consequence.

Postmodernists see debates about change and preservation as a distraction. They think fairness, justice, rationality and truth are just narrative constructs that help maintain the dominant power structures.

We can also see the signature styles of each attitude in their response to the challenges posed by VAR. The liberal doesn't see what the problem is. Indeed, they may even see VAR as a success on its own terms. It has revealed some previously unknown truths about the universe that have helped place the game on a more logical footing.

The conservative tears their hair out and gets annoyed at the blindness of the liberal, who refuses to see the bigger picture and the damage their tinkering is doing to a precious institution.

The postmodernist smiles ironically at the naivety of those who believe in any of these meta-narratives about rationality or institutions. For them, this whole debate – like all those in human affairs – is just a power play.

Liberals and conservatives alike are committed to the survival of the institution, but they will frequently accuse each other of putting it at risk by emboldening the postmodernists. The conservatives think that the liberals are too self-critical. They'll argue that constantly pointing out all the mistakes and errors in the current system undermines it. No system can ever be perfect, however brilliant the liberal reformers, and if all you focus on are the errors, you will encourage those who want to get rid of the institution completely. There is certainly some truth in the claim that historically, those reformers who have constantly focused on the weaknesses of institutions do end up becoming generally quite anti-institution and anti-authority.

However, the liberal can make a similar claim about the conservative. They will argue that it is the conservative refusal to change that actually damages the institution. Ignoring legitimate criticisms that could be easily addressed makes the system look stupid and its leaders look out of touch, and it encourages those critics who want to get rid of the institution completely. If all you focus on is the maintenance of your own authority, you will encourage the postmodernists who say that all authority is an illegitimate power grab. And there is certainly some truth in the claim that those conservatives who focus solely on preserving the authority and power of the institution often end up denying the importance of truth or rationality.

The conservative is suspicious that underneath it all, the liberal is secretly a postmodernist who doesn't care about the integrity of the institution, only about picking holes and finding faults. The liberal is suspicious that underneath it all, the conservative is secretly a postmodernist who doesn't care about the integrity of the institution, only about maintaining its power.

What about the postmodernists, who are sceptical about the idea of truth? They come in different flavours. You can be sceptical about truth in populist or academic ways.

If football were run by the populist postmodernists, it would be a tremendously exciting spectacle. The refereeing would be atrociously incompetent and horribly biased towards the powerful teams. Everyone would watch it because it was so compelling, but you would come away from it feeling unclean.

If football were run by the academic postmodernists, it would be a tremendously dull spectacle. The game would stop every minute for a five-minute review of all the footage from fifteen different angles. League table point tallies would be provisional, with confidence intervals, and subject to rolling legal challenges, statistical revisions and methodological updates. Nobody would watch it because it was so dull.

In both cases, the actual football would be a secondary consideration. The way to win trophies would not be to play better football or develop more innovative tactics. It would be to bribe (or, more politely, 'lobby') the right official or statistician.

If you are interested in resolving some of these problems, postmodernism is not going to help, whatever the flavour. But liberalism and conservatism do both have valuable insights that can help us.

Liberalism is right about change being inevitable. Young football fans have never known life without the internet. Things don't stay the same, and you need to respond to the changes. You can't keep the game in aspic. The Thierry Henry handball, the Frank Lampard ghost goal, the Carlos Tevez offside and the instant video replays of them are the strongest argument in favour of some kind of decision review system.

But conservatism is right that perfection is impossible. Completely consistent and fair refereeing decisions are impossible to achieve. No system can be fair, sensible, consistent and timely, and the pursuit of perfect fairness may lead to us sacrificing other important goals. There are no solutions, only trade-offs. The Coventry City offside, the Joachim Andersen handball and the Luis Díaz offside are the strongest arguments against the decision review system we have at the moment.

Change is inevitable. Perfection is impossible. These are central truths. They may even have the same underlying reason: that the universe is always changing, but always tending to disorder.

The conservative might also add that the search for improvement and perfection can become pathological. Let's consider that in the final chapter.

14

IDOLATRY

The old order changeth, yielding place to new.

Alfred Tennyson

I can't remember the first football match I watched on TV, because games always seemed to be on in the background. But I can remember the first rugby matches I watched. They were at the 1995 Rugby World Cup, the one where Jonah Lomu took the world by storm.

I also remember that before the tournament started, the England captain, Will Carling, caused an almighty media storm by calling the men on rugby union's ruling committee '57 old farts'. I was ten at the time, and this insult particularly appealed to my ten-year-old sense of humour. When I'd finished laughing, I asked my father why he had called them that. He said that it was because Carling wanted rugby players to be paid for playing the sport, and that the old farts did not. 'Wait a minute,' I said. 'You mean they *don't* get paid already?' 'No,' he said. 'They have other jobs. See that player, Jeremy Guscott? He works for BT. You never know, you might see him up a telegraph pole one day.'This was not true. Guscott did not work for British Telecom, nor did he climb telegraph poles for a living. He worked in PR for British Gas. But I still occasionally look at telegraph poles out of train windows and wonder if Jeremy Guscott is at the top of them.

That rugby players did not get paid for playing made no sense to me. About a year before this, Blackburn Rovers had broken the British transfer record to sign Chris Sutton from Norwich City for £5 million. It was reported in one tabloid that he was on a salary of £10,000 a week, and in another that it was £13,000. It was said elsewhere that the top players could double their salaries with boot sponsor-ship deals.

At my primary school, this was all a hot topic of discus-sion. To be a professional footballer was the great ambition of most of the boys. 'Professional' was a term of the high-est respect and approbation. You got paid to play football! You didn't have to pay money for a pair of football boots – companies *paid you* to wear their boots!

After the 1995 tournament, the old farts backed down, and it was announced that rugby union would be turning professional. Players could now be paid to play rugby. To my mind, it seemed as though the sport had finally caught up and joined the modern world.

Fifteen years later, I was teaching in a comprehensive in south-east London that was similar to the primary school I'd attended, where the pupils were just as fascinated and awestruck by the salaries and lifestyles of professional footballers as I and my classmates had been.

I taught English, and one of the GCSE coursework tasks involved students giving a solo speech to an audience. I asked one class to give speeches about something they would change if they were prime minister for the day. A pupil called James decided the one thing he would change would be to pay footballers less, because he thought they earnt too much.

James was a Charlton Athletic season-ticket holder and a huge fan of most sports. But in his speech, he argued that footballers were overpaid. It was crazy that so many of them earned millions of pounds a year just for kicking a ball around a pitch. One point he repeated a couple of times was that it was absurd that they earnt more than firefighters and nurses, who did such important, life-saving jobs. It was a good speech, engaging and thought-provoking, and it certainly captured the attention of his audience. When he mentioned firefighters and nurses, there were nods of agreement around the room and murmurs of approval.

When he had finished, I decided to ask the first question.

'Who, in your opinion, is the third-best goalkeeper in League One?'

He looked a little surprised at this question, but gave it some thought and replied.

'Who is the best teenager in League One?'

He replied again, quicker this time.

'OK,' I said. 'Who is the third-best firefighter in the south-east London firefighting division?'

He looked blank and slightly confused.

'What about the best up-and-coming nurse in your local NHS Trust?'

He still looked blank. I put my head in my hands. 'This is it, James,' I said. 'Don't you get it? Of course it's absurd that footballers get paid so much. Of course there is a problem. But *you* are the problem!'

Now he was looking really confused and slightly worried. I realised I might be being a bit harsh.

'Not just you, of course,' I said. '*We* are the problem. *I* am the problem. This all happens because of *us.*'

Now the whole class were looking at me. I decided we could finish the question-and-answer session there, and that James could have an A*.

In *City of God*, the Christian St Augustine argues that many of the woes we face are the result of getting our priorities wrong. The term most of the translations use is that we have 'disordered loves'. A virtuous person is one who orders their loves in a sensible fashion. An unvirtuous person does not.

We all know it's a bad thing to enjoy bad things. What

Augustine also points out, though, is that it is a bad thing to enjoy good things too much.

I think this is the point that the 57 old farts and James are, in different ways, trying to make. They like sport, and they think it's a good thing. But they also think it can get out of all proportion. In the end, it is just a game. There are more important things in life, and there are people who do more important jobs.

My mother makes a similar point. Unlike James and the old farts, she does not like sport, and I suspect she would happily live in a world without it. But she knows to check the West Ham scores when my father and I are at the football, and when she sees we are losing, she will text us both: 'At least you've still got me.' It has now become a joke between me and my dad. We will be sitting there waiting for the latest VAR check, and he'll say, 'Never mind. We've still got your mother.' Of course, the old farts would go further than James and my mother, and their ancestors, the public-school men of the late 19th century who laid down so many of the conventions of modern sport, would go further still.

They would say that not only should sport not be about money, it should not be about entertainment, either. It should be designed for the average participant, not for the spectator or the elite player. It should be about building character, and very much about the taking part, not the winning. Nor should it crowd out more meaningful pursuits. If you have a talent for sport but also have one that could help society, you should consider giving up the serious pursuit of sport to devote yourself to the greater good.

Many of these men would have read their St Augustine and agreed that sport could easily become idolatrous. Augustine's point was that our earthly loves should not be an end in themselves, but a means through which we reach God.

Arthur Conan Doyle quite explicitly made a similar argument during the Boer War. The conflict went on for longer than many people had anticipated and persisted into 1901, when a South African cricket team was scheduled to tour England. Conan Doyle reacted with anger when he heard the tour was still going ahead:

> When our young men are going from North to South to fight for the cause of South Africa, these South Africans are coming from South to North to play cricket. It is a stain on their manhood that they are not out with rifles in their hands driving the invader from their country. They leave this to others while they play games. There may be some question even in England whether the national game has justified itself during this crisis, and whether cricketers have shown that they understood that the only excuse for a game is that it keeps a man fit for the serious duties of life.[22]

'The only excuse for a game is that it keeps a man fit for the serious duties of life.' That is the authentic voice of the 19th-century amateur. What would Conan Doyle and his type make of modern sport?

Let's make the case for them. Modern sport features a tiny number of elite, overpaid athletes who have made sporting success their sole goal in life. Their every whim is indulged, and they are excused from many of the accepted standards of life, so long as their performance is good. In return for this, many of them are expected to reach freakish physical standards, which may damage their health in the long term. Sportsmen and -women are locked in an exhausting arms race where they must always be alert for the next innovation, the next advance, the next means of gaining an edge over the competition.

They are watched and enabled by vast armies of demanding fans who themselves mostly do very little exercise and in many cases are unhealthily overweight. Fans and players lack respect for the game's authorities, while the authorities themselves make no attempt to enforce a moral code, but are instead happy to indulge whichever of the fans' whims will make them the most money.

It's often assumed that the 19th-century amateur would reserve most of their scorn for football, with its vulgar embrace of big money. But I think they would be just as appalled by some of the more middle-class sports. Cycling, for instance: I suspect many of them would view David

Brailsford's 'aggregation of marginal gains' strategy with horror. The idea that the way to do well in sport is to travel with a custom-made pillow and wear electrically heated overshorts would have been anathema to them.

The 19th-century amateurs are often accused of hypocrisy, but I think they would laugh at *our* hypocrisy in banning drugs from sport. You let all *this* happen, they would say, and yet you draw the line at drugs? Why? If you are going to have a free-for-all, then go the whole way and have a free-for-all! You laughed at us for trying to hold the line against what you said was inevitable; well, now we will laugh at you as you try to hold the line against drugs in sport, which are quite obviously an inevitable, logical consequence of what you have enabled.

And, of course, they would laugh hollowly at VAR too. This, they would say, is your punishment for your pursuit of greed and your disordered love. If you want a vision of the professional game's future, imagine Harry Kane's boot being VAR-checked – forever.

The reality, they would say, is that far from trying to eliminate the bad refereeing decision, you should welcome it, because the errors are a chance for us to learn fortitude and self-control in the face of the inevitable slings and arrows of life.

When I think of James and his firefighter argument, when I read St Augustine and when I imagine the ghost of the 19th-century amateur, I think, you know what, there is a lot of truth to all this. Modern sport is mad. Arguing over offside is mad. Devoting significant intellectual energy to making sporting decisions marginally more accurate is a textbook case of idolatry. Our loves are disordered, our priorities are back to front, we worship what we should use and we use what we should worship.

But I never think it for very long. As St Augustine also said, we are all fallen creatures, and we live in a fallen world. And the fallen world we inhabit at the moment is one where we need a solution to VAR.

NOTES

1 BBC Sport, 'VAR in the Premier League: How Did First
   Weekend Go for Technology in Top Flight?' BBC Sport, 11
   August 2019. https://www.bbc.co.uk/sport/football/
   49307496.

2 Ibid.

3 Ziegler, Martyn, 'VAR Has Made Football More Fair, Says
   David Elleray', *The Times*, 17 December 2020. https://www.
   thetimes.com/sport/football/article/var-has-made-football-
   more-fair-says-david-elleray-jbz6pzwlg.

4 Sharpe, James, 'What a VARce: Premier League Accused of
   "Lowering Bar for Clear and Obvious" and Liverpool Players
   Call for Video Assistant Referee to Be Scrapped Following
   Late Controversy at Brighton', *Daily Mail*, 28 November 2020.
   https://www.dailymail.co.uk/sport/football/article-8996913/
   Premier-League-accused-changing-rules-Liverpool-players-
   call-VAR-scrapped.

5 Caruso, E. M., Burns, Z. C. and Converse, B. A., 'Slow Motion Increases Perceived Intent', *Proceedings of the National
   Academy of Sciences of the United States of America*, 113 (33)

(2016), pp. 9250–5. https://doi.org/10.1073/pnas.1603865113.

6   Spitz, Jochim, et al., 'The Impact of Video Speed on the Decision-Making Process of Sports Officials', *Cognitive Research: Principles and Implications*, vol. 3 (2018), pp. 1–10.

7   Chowdhury, Saj, 'VAR: "Armpit Offsides" Strike Again in the Premier League', BBC Sport, 28 December 2019. https://www.bbc.co.uk/sport/football/50935709.

8   Ibid.

9   Ibid.

10 Wilson, Jonathan, 'Why Is the Modern Offside Law a Work of Genius?' *Guardian*, 13 April 2010. https://www.theguardian.com/sport/blog/2010/apr/13/the-question-why-is-offside-law-genius.

11 Vice, Telford, 'How Cricket Built a Healthy, and Evolving, Relationship with Electronic Umpiring', 25 April 2024. https://telfordvice.wordpress.com/2024/04/25/how-cricket-built-a-healthy-and-evolving-relationship-with-electronic-umpiring.

12 Reason, James, 'Human Error: Models and Management', *British Medical Journal*, 320.7237 (2000), pp. 768–70.

13 Haidt, Jonathan, *The Righteous Mind: Why Good People Are Divided by Politics and Religion*. Vintage, 2012, p. 73.

14 Dawkins, Richard, 'The Tyranny of the Discontinuous Mind', *New Statesman*, 19 December 2011. https://www.newstatesman.com/politics/2011/12/issue-essay-line-dawkins.

15 Kuhn, Thomas S., 'Second Thoughts on Paradigms', in *The Essential Tension: Selected Studies in Scientific Tradition and Change*. University of Chicago Press, 2011, p. 305.

16 Ibid, p. 307.

17 Brettig, Daniel, '"Shocking and Embarrassing" System May Be Short-Lived', ESPN Cricinfo, 15 November 2012. https://www.espncricinfo.com/story/shocking-and-embarrassing-third-umpire-interventions-may-be-short-lived-591378.

18 'Playing by Laboratory Rules', *Wales Online*, 14 February 2004. https://www.walesonline.co.uk/news/wales-news/playing-by-laboratory-rules-2449860.

19 Ibid.

20 USA Facts Team, 'Is Flying Safer Than Driving?' *USA Facts*, 19 December 2023. https://usafacts.org/articles/is-flying-safer-than-driving.

21 Nesse, Randolph M., *Good Reasons for Bad Feelings: Insights from the Frontier of Evolutionary Psychiatry*. Penguin, 2019, p. 38.

22 Conan Doyle, Arthur, Letter in *The Spectator*, no. 3799, 20 April 1901.

ACKNOWLEDGEMENTS

TK